HUNGARIAN SELF – TAUGHT

Marlborough's Self-Taught Series

HUNGARIAN SELF – TAUGHT

**By the Natural Method
with
Phonetic Pronunciation**

**BY
THE COUNT DE SOISSONS**

Revised by

MRS. ILONA DE GYORY GINEVER

THIRD EDITION

GYAN

Published by

Gyan Publishing House
5, Ansari Road
Daryaganj, New Delhi-110002
Phone: 011-47034999, 9811692060
E-mail: books@gyanbooks.com

Distribution Network
gyanbooks.com
India, USA, Canada, UK, Australia, France

ISBN : 978-81-212-4429-9 (PB)

2nd Impression 2020

Printed at: Gyan Press, Delhi.

Hungarian Self - Taught
Author: Mrs. Ilona De Gyory Ginever

Marlborough's Self-Taught Series

Hungarian Self-Taught

by the Natural Method

WITH

Phonetic Pronunciation

TRADE MARK ST SERIES REGISTERED

BY

The COUNT de SOISSONS

Revised by

Mrs. ILONA DE GYÖRY GINEVER

THIRD EDITION

PRINTED IN GREAT BRITAIN

LONDON PUBLISHERS : E. MARLBOROUGH & Co. LTD.

PHILADELPHIA :

DAVID McKAY COMPANY, PUBLISHERS,

604-608, SOUTH WASHINGTON SQUARE.

PREFACE.

THE publication of *Hungarian Self-Taught* marks the inclusion of a new group of languages in the "Self-Taught Series," Hungarian being akin to the languages of the Finns, Lapps, and certain tribes in Russia and Siberia, whilst standing quite apart from the Latin, German, Scandinavian and other groups.

The main purpose of this manual is to facilitate the speedy acquisition of a working and practical knowledge of Hungarian, as far as possible without the usual long and tedious operation of mastering the Grammar, which many persons find it impracticable or distasteful to undertake, to whom, nevertheless, some acquaintance with the spoken tongue is necessary, or at least advantageous, for the purposes of commerce or of travel and pleasure.

The book chiefly consists, therefore, of a large number of comprehensive Vocabularies, and collections of idiomatic Conversational Phrases and Sentences, such as are required for every-day use, carefully selected and classified according to subject. The words in each vocabulary are placed in alphabetical order, and there are cross-references between the vocabularies and the corresponding groups of sentences.

The matter is arranged in three columns, viz., first the English words or sentences, then the Hungarian translation, and third, the phonetic pronunciation of the Hungarian words. In the conversations the aim has been to give the colloquial equivalent in Hungarian, rather than the literal translation of the English. The pronunciation given in the third column is in accordance with Marlborough's system of phonetics. This system is the outcome of long experience, and is of so simple a nature that it enables anyone who knows English, however strange to the Hungarian language, to read off the words at a glance, and easily make himself understood amongst Hungarians, with the minimum of trouble in mastering the system.

The first section of the book, dealing with the Alphabet and pronunciation, provides the scheme of phonetics adopted in this volume, and in the introductory paragraphs thereto the principles upon which the scheme is based are explained, and particular attention is drawn to the phonetic signs employed to represent the few sounds which are more or less unfamiliar to the English ear.

For the benefit of students and others who desire to become more closely acquainted with Hungarian, a very full outline of the Grammar is added, followed by a section on Etymology, and thus the way is opened to the thorough study and mastery of the language.

To commercial men, tourists, travellers, students, and all who desire to enter into communication with the Hungarians, this work will prove a useful and valuable handbook of the language. Students will, moreover, find that the book forms an easy introduction to a language which has a quaint beauty of its own, and possesses a remarkable literature, rich especially in heroic poetry.

SOISSONS.

London, 1910

CONTENTS.

	Page
THE ALPHABET, with Phonetic Pronunciation	7
PRELIMINARY NOTES—Pronunciation, Accents, Vowels, Prolongation of the Vowels...	9
VOCABULARIES—Pages 11–66.	
Amusements	39
Animals, Vegetables, etc. :—	
Animals, Birds and Fishes	14
Fruits, Trees, Flowers and Vegetables	17
Reptiles and Insects	16
Colours	19
Commercial and Trading Terms	49
Cooking and Eating Utensils	31
Correspondence	53
Countries and Nations	38
Cycling	42
House and Furniture	34
Legal Terms	47
Mankind: Relations	23
Human Body, The	25
Dress and the Toilet	31
Food and Drink	29
Health	28
Physical and Mental Powers, Qualities, etc.	26
Numbers—Cardinal, Ordinal, Collective	53–55
Parts of Speech	55–66
Adjectives	55
Adverbs, Conjunctions and Prepositions	63
Verbs	59
Photography	44
Post-office, Telegraph and Telephone	52
Professions and Trades	46
Religion	45
Times, Seasons and Holidays	19
Town and Country	22
Travelling	36
Travelling by Ship	37
Washing List	33
World and its Elements, The	11
Land and Water	12
Minerals and Metals	13

CONTENTS

	Page
ELEMENTARY GRAMMAR—Pages 67–82.	
The Adjective	70
„ Adverb	82
„ Article	67
„ Conjunction	81
„ Interjection	82
„ Postposition	69
„ Pronoun	71
„ Substantive	67
„ Verb	73
ETYMOLOGY	83
MODES OF ADDRESS	84
CONVERSATIONAL PHRASES AND SENTENCES—Pages 85–110.	
Amusements	100
Commercial and Trading	109
Correspondence	107
Cycling	101
Enquiries	87
Expressions, Idiomatic, Useful and Necessary	85
Expressions of Emotion	87
Health	95
Legal and Judicial Phrases	108
Meals:—Breakfast, Dinner and Tea	92–94
Money Changing	110
Photography	102
Post, Telegraph and Telephone	106
Religion	103
Shopping	97
Dressmaker	98
Shoemaker	98
Laundress	99
Time of Day, The	104
Times, Seasons and Weather	105
Town, In	95
Travelling:—	
Arrival	91
Changing Money	110
Custom House, At the	91
Hotel	92
Notices	88
Railway	88
Steamboat	90
Useful and Necessary Expressions	85
MONEY, Hungarian, with English and American values	111
„ English and American, reduced to Hungarian	111
WEIGHTS AND MEASURES	111
POSTAL RATES	112

HUNGARIAN SELF-TAUGHT.

The Alphabet, with Phonetic Pronunciation.

The principle on which Marlborough's system of phonetics is based may be stated briefly as "One sign, one sound," and conversely "One sound, one sign."

The student should constantly bear this principle in mind, and pronounce each of the phonetics employed in this volume *always* in the same manner.

Attention is particularly drawn, therefore, to the phonetic use of a, e, i, and o, which, in the third column throughout the Vocabularies and Conversations, represent the short vowel sounds in at, et, it, ot, respectively. Other phonetic signs to be noted are ĕ*r* and e*r* (short and long respectively), ŏŏ, e͡u, ĭu, d*y*, and zh.

The Hungarian language has the following single letters:—

Characters.	Name and English Pronunciation.	Phonetics used.
A, a	(ah) like *a* in *watch* or *o* in *not*:—*farkas* (forrkosh), wolf	o
Á, á	(ah) like *a* in *far*:—*leány* (le-ahny*), girl	ah
B, b	(beh) as in English:—*ablak* (oblok), window	b
C, c	(tseh) like *ts* in *its*:—*citrom* (tsitrom), lemon	ts
D, d	(deh) as in English:—*dárda* (dahrrdo*), spear	d
E, e	(eh) like *a* in *bad*†:—*nem* (nam), no	a *or* e
É, é	(eh) like *a* in *fate*:—*pénz* (pehnz), money	eh
F, f	(ef) as in English:—*fa* (fo*), tree	f
G, g	(geh) like *g* in *gag*:—*görbe* (ghe*r*rbe*), crooked	g, gh
H, h	(hah) like *h* in *house*:—*háború* (hahborroo), war	h
I, i	(ee) like *i* in *pitch*:—*iga* (ig-o*) yoke	i
Í, í	(ee) like *i* in *machine*:—*ív* (eev), arch	ee
J, j	(yeh) like *y*:—*jó* (yoh), good; *héja* (hehyo), hawk	y

* Pronounce a, e, i, and o ALWAYS as if followed by a consonant in the same syllable. (See third paragraph above.)

† Sometimes like *e* in *bed*, especially in the case of words in which *e* occurs more than once; e.g. *engem* (pronounced angem).

Characters.	Name and English Pronunciation.	Phonetics used.
K, k ...	(kah) as in English :—*katona* (kotono*), soldier...	k
L, l ...	(ehl) as in English :—*liba* (lib-o*), goose... ...	l
M, m...	(em) as in English :—*malom* (molom), mill ...	m
N, n ...	(en) as in English :—*néni* (nehni), elder sister ...	n
O, o ...	(oh) like *o* in *fort* :—*okos* (okosh), prudent ...	o
Ó, ó ...	(oh) like *o* in *goal* :—*óra* (ohrro), hour	oh
Ö, ö ...	(oh) like *ea* in *earth* (short), or *eu* in the French *neuf* :—*öreg* (ĕrreg), old	†ĕr
Ő, ő ...	(oh) like ö, but longer, i.e. like *u* in *fur*, *œu* in the French *sœur* :—*bőr* (berr), skin	†er
P, p ...	(peh) as in English :—*párna* (pahrno), cushion ...	p
R, r ...	(ehr) like *rr* in *barren* ; must always be clearly sounded :—*ritka* (ritko), rare	r, rr
S, s ...	(ash) like *sh* in *shoe* :—*sas* (shosh), eagle	sh
T, t ...	(teh) as in English :—*tudni* (tŏŏdni*), to know ...	t
U, u ...	(oo) like *u* in *bull* :—*futni* (fŏŏtni), to run ...	ŏŏ
Ú, ú ...	(oo) like *oo* in *food* :—*rút* (root), ugly	oo
Ü, ü ...	(eu) like *u* in the French *juste* :—*fül* (fe͡ul), ear ...	‡e͡u
Ű, ű ...	(eu) sometimes like *u* in *duty* (very soft), or *eu* in the French *morue* :—*tűz* (tīuz), fire	īu
V, v ...	(veh) as in English : *várni* (vahrni), to wait ...	v
X, x ...	(iks) as in English (not usual in Hungarian) :— *xylograph* (xylogrof)	x
Y, y ...	(eepseelon) as in English : only occurs in names	y
Z, z ...	(zeh) as in English :—*zene* (zan-a*), music ...	z

Besides single letters Hungarian has some double ones, each of which, however, represents a single sound and cannot be divided in pronunciation or spelling :—

Cs ...	(cheh) like *ch* in *church*:—*csuda* (chŏŏdo), wonder	ch *or* tch
Cz§...	(tseh-zeh) like *ts* in *its* :—*czél* (tsehl), aim	ts
Ds ...	(jeh) like *j* in *joke* :—*findsa* (finjo), cup	j
Gy ...	(dyey) like *d* in *dew* (very soft):—*gyűrű* (dyīurīu), ring	dy

[There is a *y* sound added to the *d* sound, as in the *dy* in *Goodyear* or *Rudyard*, and the *di* in *adieu* pronounced as in France.]

* See footnote on preceding page. † Pronounce ĕr and er as *er* in *over* and *herb* respectively, without sounding the *r*. ‡ Form the lips as for whistling and pronounce eu as one sound. § Cz is now very largely replaced by C, the pronunciation being the same. This spelling is adopted throughout this book.

Characters.	Name and English Pronunciation.	Phonetics used.
Ly ...	(ehl-eepseelon) like *y* in *you*:—*ilyen* (iyen), such ...	y, y'
Ny...	(ain) something like *ny* in *Bunyan*, or like *gne* in the French *campagne*:—*nyúl* (nyool), hare	ny
Sz ...	(ass) like *s* in *servant*:—*szem* (sam), eye	s, ss
Ty*...	(tyeh) like *t-y* in *not‿you*:—*tyúk* (tyook), hen ...	ty
Zs ...	(zseh) like *z* in *azure*:—*zsir* (zhirr), lard	zh
Dzs...	(jeh) like *j* in *joke*:—*dzsida* (jido), spear	j

PRELIMINARY NOTES.

Pronunciation.—The Hungarian language requires clear and distinct articulation; two consonants (whether single or double), coming together, must each be distinctly sounded.†

If *j* follows *ny*, *ty*, it is pronounced as if the *n* or *t* were doubled, *nny*, *tty*, as *anyja* (on-nyo) his mother, *atyja* (ot-tyo) his father.

When a consonant is doubled it must be pronounced doubly, and a slight stress must be laid on the first syllable; e.g. *villa*, fork; *szappan*, soap.

One must be careful to make a difference in pronouncing long and short vowels, for often the meaning of a word depends on the pronunciation of *a* or *á*, of *o* or *ó*, *ö*, *ő*, of *ü* or *ű*; as *hat* (hot), six, *hát* (haht), back; *kor* (korr), age, *kór* (kohr), illness.

Tonic Accent.—In Hungarian each word has **as many syllables** as it contains **vowels**; as *leányaié*=le-ahn-yo-i-eh. The spoken or **tonic accent is always on the first syllable**, be it the root or prefix, long or short.

Accents.—There are the following accents: ', ¨, ″. They are used to indicate the varying pronunciation of certain vowels, as shown in the Alphabet.

* *Ty* is the sharp articulation of *gy*. These two sounds are the most difficult; they are in the same relation to each other as the English syllables "du" and "tu" in the words "due" and "tube."

† It may be remarked that, orthographically, instead of the double consonants *gygy*, *lyly*, *nyny*, *tyty*, *cscs*, *czcz*, *szsz*, the forms *ggy*, *lly*, *nny*, *tty*, *ccs*, *ccz*, *ssz* are used. However, if *gy*, *ly*, *ny*, *ty*, *cs*, *cz*, *sz* are at the ends of the words, and the final consonant must be doubled on account of suffix, one must write: *ágygyal*, with the bed, *őszszel*, in autumn. etc.

The Vowels.—In Hungarian the different relations between the parts of speech, the conjugations of verbs, the gradation of adjectives, and the possessive case, are expressed by means of suffixes added to the root (which never changes); as *asztal*, table, *asztal-ok*, tables, *asztal-om*, my table; *szeret-ni*, to love, *szeret-ünk*, we love, *szeret-tünk*, we have loved; *magas*, high, *magas-abb*, higher.

For this reason the dominating rule is harmony, which demands that the suffix must sound like the vowels in the root. Consequently, the vowels are divided into SHORT, *a*, *e*, *i*, *o*, *õ*, *u*, *ü*, and LONG, *á*, *é*, *í*, *ó*, *ő*, *ú*, *ű*. These are again subdivided into FLAT, *a*, *á*. *o*, *ó*, *u*, *ú*; SHARP, *e*, *ö*, *ő*, *ü*, *ű*; and MEDIATE, *é*, *i*, *í*. The sharp vowels demand sharp suffixes, whilst the flat and mediate ones require flat and mediate suffixes respectively.

When the same word contains vowels of two different classes, the sharp vowels are considered as the principal ones, and the word belongs to the class of sharp words. Sometimes, however, the vowel of the last syllable commands the suffix of the same character.

The choice of the suffix always depends on the vowel of the root, as *ház*, house; *ház-ak*, houses; *ház-nak*, to the house; *ház-ban*, in the house; *ház-am*, my house. On the contrary, *kert*, garden; *kert-ek*, gardens; *kert-nek*, to the garden; *kert-ben*, in the garden; *kert-em*, my garden, etc.

When the demonstrative pronoun *az* (that), *ez* (this), joins the suffixes, which are used instead of prepositions, its consonant *z* is assimilated to the initial consonant of the suffix; as *ar-ról*, of that, instead of *az-ról*; *eb-ből*, out of this, instead of *ez-ből*.

The affixes *val*, *vel*, which express the preposition "with," and *vá*, *vé*, which means "into," assimilate their initial consonant *v* to the final consonant of the word to which they are joined; thus, *kéz-zel*, with the hand, instead of *kéz-vel*.

Prolongation of the Vowels.—The short final vowels *a* and *e* are prolonged as often as the word assumes any affix. This prolongation is common to all words in all grammatical forms; *ruha*, dress, *ruhá-m*, my dress, *ruhá-t*, a dress (objective case), *ruhá-zni*, to dress, etc.; and it extends even so far that, if affixes which terminate with a short *e* or *a* receive any other affixes whatsoever, the short *e* or *a* of the former is accentuated; as *ruha*, dress, *ruhá-ja*, his dress, *ruhá-já-val*, with his dress.

VOCABULARIES.

The World and its Elements.

(*A világ és elemei.*)

English.	Hungarian.	Pronunciation.
The air	*a levegő*	o* lavag-er
the cloud	*a felhő*	o falher
the cold	*a hideg*	o hid-ag
the darkness	*a sötétség*	o shĕrtehtshehg
the dew	*a harmat*	o horrmot
the dust	*a por*	o porr
the earth	*a föld*	o fĕrld
east	*kelet*	kal-at
an eclipse †	*fogyatkozás*	fod*y*otkozahsh
the fire	*a tűz*	o tüuz
the fog	*a köd*	o kĕrd
the frost	*a fagy*	o fod*y*
the hail	*a jégeső*	o yehg-ash-er
the heat	*a hőség*	o hershehg
the light	*a világosság*	o vilahgosh-shahg
the lightning	*a villámlás*	o villahmlahsh
the moon	*a hold*	o hold (hol *as in* hollow)
—, full	*telihold*	tal-i-hold
—, new	*újhold*	ooy hold
moonlight	*holdvilág*	holdvilahg
nature	*természet*	terrmehsat
north	*észak*	ehsok
the rainbow	*a szivárvány*	o sivahrr-vahn*y*
shade, a shadow	*az árnyék*	oz ahrr-n*y*ehk
the sky	*az égboltozat*	oz ehgboltozot
south	*dél*	dehl
the star	*a csillag*	o chillog
the sun	*a nap*	o nop
the thunder	*a dörgés*	o dĕrr-ghehsh
the weather	*az időjárás*	oz ideryahrrahsh
west	*nyugat*	nyŏŏgot
the wind	*a szél*	o sehl

* Pronounce *o* as in *not*. † The indefinite article is usually omitted in Hungarian; see p. 67. Regarding gender, see p. 84.

Land and Water. (*Föld és víz.*)

English.	Hungarian.	Pronunciation.
A bay	*öböl*	ĕrbĕrl
the beach	*a part*	o porrt
the canal	*a (mű) csatorna*	o (mīu) chotorrno
the cape	*a fok*	o fok
the cliff	*a szikla*	o siklo
the coast	*a partvidék*	o porrtvidehk
the current	*az áramlat*	oz ahrromlot
the ebb	*az apály*	oz opah-y'
the flow, rising tide	*az ár*	oz ahrr
the foam	*a hab*	o hob
the hill	*a domb*	o domb
the ice	*a jég*	o yehg
an island	*sziget*	sig-at
the lake	*a tó*	o toh
the land	*a föld*	o fĕrld
the mainland	*a szárazföld*	o sahrrozfĕrld
the moor	*a zsombék*	o zhombehk
the mountain	*a hegy*	o hady
the mud	*a sár*	o shahrr
a peninsula	*félsziget*	fehlsig-at
the rain	*az eső*	oz asher
the river	*a folyó*	o foyoh
a rock	*szikla*	siklo
the sand	*a homok*	o homok
the sea	*a tenger*	o tan-gherr
the sea-shore	*a tengerpart*	o tan-gherrporrt
the shingle	*a kavics*	o kov-itch
the snow	*a hó*	o hoh
a storm	*vihar*	vihorr
the thaw	*az olvadás*	oz olvodahsh
the tide	*az ár*	oz ahrr
at high tide	*dagály (ár)*	dogah-y' (ahrr)
at low tide	*apály*	opah-y'
the water	*a víz*	o veez
fresh water	*édesvíz*	ehdashveez
salt water	*sósvíz*	shohsh-veez
a waterfall	*vízesés*	veezashehsh
the wave	*a hullám*	o hŏŏllahm
a well	*kút*	koot

Minerals and Metals. *(Ásványok és fémek.)*

English.	Hungarian.	Pronunciation.
The agate	*az agát*	oz ogaht
the alum	*a timsó*	o timshoh
the amber	*a borostyánkő*	o borrosht-yahnker
brass	*sárgaréz*	shahrrgorrehz
bronze	*bronz*	bronz
the carbuncle	*a kárbunkulus*	kahrrbŏŏnkŏŏlŏŏsh
the cement	*a cement*	o tsam-ant
the chalk	*a kréta, mész*	o krehto, mehss
the clay	*az agyag*	oz od-yog
the coal	*a kőszén*	o kersehn
the copper	*a vörösréz*	o vĕrrĕrshrehz
the coral	*a korall*	o korroll
the crystal	*a kristály*	o krishtah-y'
the diamond	*a gyémánt*	o dyehmahnt
the emerald	*a smaragd*	o shmorrogd
the glass	*az üveg*	oz e͡uvag
the gold	*az arany*	oz orrony
the granite	*a gránit*	o grahnit
the gravel	*a kavicsföld*	o kovichfĕrld
the iron	*a vas*	o vosh
—, cast	*az öntött vas*	oz ĕrntĕrt vosh
—, wrought	*a kovácsolt vas*	o kovahcholt vosh
the lead	*az ólom*	oz ohlom
the lime	*a mész*	o mehss
the marble	*a márvány*	o mahrrvahny
the mercury	*a kéneső, higany*	o kehnasher, higony
the metals	*a fémek*	o fehmak
mortar	*a vakolat*	o vokolot
nickel	*nikkel*	nik-kel
the opal	*az opál*	oz opahl
the pearl	*a gyöngy*	o dyĕrndy
a ruby	*rubín*	rŏŏbeen
the sapphire	*a zafír*	o zofeerr
the silver	*az ezüst*	oz aze͡usht
soda	*szíksó*	seekshoh
the steel	*az acél*	oz otsehl
the stone	*a kő*	o ker
the tin	*az ón*	oz ohn
the zinc	*a horgany*	o horrgony

Animals, Birds, and Fishes.

(*Emlősök,* madarak és halak.*)

(For Shopping, see p. 97.)

English.	Hungarian.	Pronunciation.
An animal	*állat*	ahl-lot
barking	*az ugatás*	oz ŏŏgot-ahsh
a bear	*medve*	madva
a bird	*madár*	modahrr
a blackbird	*fekete rigó*	fak-a-ta rigoh
bleating	*a bégetés*	o behgatehsh
braying	*az ordítás*	oz orrditahsh
a bull	*bika*	biko
a calf	*borjú*	borr-yoo
a carp	*ponty*	ponty
the cat	*a macska*	o motchko
a chicken	*csirke*	o chirrka
the claw	*a karom*	o korrom
a cock	*kakas*	kok-osh
a cod	*gadóc*	god-ohts
the colt	*a csikó*	o chikoh
a cow	*tehén*	ta-hehn
a crab	*rák*	rahk
the crow	*a varjú*	o vorr-yoo
a cuckoo	*kakuk*	kok-ŏŏk
the dog	*a kutya*	o kŏŏt-yo
a donkey	*szamár*	som-ahrr
the dove	*a galamb*	o gol-omb
a duck	*kacsa*	kotcho
a wild duck	*vadkacsa*	vodkotcho
the eagle	*a sas*	o shosh
an eel	*angolna*	on-golno
an elephant	*elefánt*	al-a-fahnt
a feather	*toll*	tol (*like* doll)
the fins	*az úszók*	oz oosohk
a fish	*hal*	hol
the fox	*a róka*	o rohko
the fur	*a prém*	o prehm
the gills	*a kopoltyúk*	o kopolt-yook
a goat	*kecske*	katch-ka
a goose	*liba*	libo

* *Emlősök* means "mammals," to which meaning "animals" is here limited.

English.	Hungarian.	Pronunciation.
a gull	*sirály*	shirrah-y'
a haddock	*tőkehal*	terka-hol
the hair	*a haj, a szőr*	o hoy, o serr
the hare	*a nyúl*	o nyool
a hawk	*héja*	heyo
a hen	*tyúk*	tyook
a herring	*hering*	herring
the hoof, nail	*a pata*	o pot-o
the horn	*a szarv*	o sorrv
a horse	*ló*	loh
the howling	*az üvöltés*	oz e͡uvĕrltehsh
a lamb	*bárány*	bahrrahny
a lark	*pacsirta*	potchirrto
a lion	*oroszlán*	orrosslahn
a lobster	*tengeri rák*	tan-gherri rahk
a mackerel	*makár*	mok-ahrr
a magpie	*szarka*	sorrko
the mane	*a sörény*	o shĕrrehny
the mewing	*a nyávogás*	o nyahvogahsh
a monkey	*majom*	moyom
the mouse	*az egér*	oz ag-ehrr
a mullet	*a fejes bömbösz*	o feyash bĕrmbĕrss
neighing	*nyerités*	nyereetehsh
a nightingale	*csalogány*	chol-o-gahny
an owl	*bagoly*	bogoy
an ox	*ökör*	ĕrkĕrr
the oyster	*az osztriga*	oz ostrigo
the parrot	*a papagály*	o popogah-y'
a partridge	*fogoly*	fogoy
the paw	*a mancs*	o monch
the peacock	*a páva*	o pahvo
the pheasant	*a fácán*	o fahtsahn
a pig	*disznó*	dissnoh
a pigeon	*galamb*	golomb
a pike	*csuka*	chŏŏko
the plaice	*a tarsony*	o torrshony
a quail	*fürj*	fe͡urr-y'
the rabbit	*a tengeri nyúl*	o tan-gherri nyool
the rat	*a patkány*	o potkahny
the raven	*a holló*	o holloh
a salmon	*lazac*	lozots

English.	Hungarian.	Pronunciation.
the scales	*a pikkelyek*	o pikkeyak
a sheep	*birka, juh*	birrko, yŏŏh
the snipe	*a sárszalonka*	o shahrr-solonko
the sparrow	*a veréb*	o verrehb
the stork	*a gólya*	o goh-yo
the swallow	*a fecske*	o fatchka
a swan	*hattyú*	hott-yoo
the tail	*a fark*	o forrk
a thrush	*sárgarigó*	shahrrgo-rigoh
a tiger	*tigris*	tig-rish
the tortoise	*a teknősbéka*	o taknershbehko
a trout	*pisztráng*	pistrahng
a turbot	*félszegúszó*	fehlsagoosoh
a turkey	*pulyka*	pŏŏy-ko
the turtle	*a tengeri teknősbéka*	o tan-gherri taknersh [behko
a whale	*cethal*	tsat-hol
a whiting	*keszeg*	kassag
a wing	*szárny*	sahrrny
a wolf	*farkas*	forrkosh
a woodpecker	*harkály*	horrkah-y'
a wood-pigeon	*vadgalamb*	vodgolomb
the wool	*a gyapjú*	o dyop-yoo
the wren	*az ökörszem*	oz ĕrkĕrrsam

Reptiles and Insects. (*Hüllők és rovarok.*)

English.	Hungarian.	Pronunciation.
An ant	*hangya*	hond-yo
a bee	*méh*	meh
a beetle	*bogár*	bogahrr
a bug	*poloska*	poloshko
a butterfly	*lepke*	lapka
a caterpillar	*hernyó*	herr-nyoh
a flea	*bolha*	bol-ho
a fly	*légy*	lehdy
a frog	*béka*	behko
a gnat	*szunyog*	sŏŏn-yog
the grasshopper	*a szöcske*	o sĕrtchka
the honey	*a méz*	o mehz
an insect	*rovar*	rovorr
a moth	*moly*	moy
a serpent, snake	*kigyó*	kid-yoh
a silkworm	*selyem-hernyó*	sheyam-herr-nyoh

English.	Hungarian.	Pronunciation.
a snail	*csiga*	chigo
a spider	*pók*	pohk
a sting	*fulánk*	föölahnk
a toad	*varangyos béka*	vorrond-yosh behko
a viper	*vipera*	viperro
a wasp	*darázs*	dorrahzh
the wax	*a viasz*	o vioss
a worm	*féreg*	fehrag

Fruits, Trees, Flowers and Vegetables.

(*Gyümölcsök, fák, virágok és zöldségek.*)

(For Shopping see page 97.)

An apple	*alma*	olmo
an ash	*kőrisfa*	kerrishfo
the asparagus	*a spárga*	o shpahrrgo
a banana	*banán*	bon-ahn
the beans	*a bab*	o bob
the beech-tree	*a bükkfa*	o beukkfo
the beetroot	*a cékla*	o tsehklo
the birch (tree)	*a nyírfa*	o nyeerrfo
a blackberry	*hamvas szeder*	homvosh sad-err
a bouquet	*bokréta*	bokrehto
a branch	(*fa*) *ág*	(fo) ahg
the cabbage	*a kelkáposzta*	o kalkahposto
the carrot	*a sárga répa*	o shahrrgo rehpo
the cauliflower	*a karfiol*	o korrfiol
the celery	*a zeller*	o zal-lerr
a cherry	*cseresznye*	cherassnya
a chestnut (edible)	*gesztenye*	gas-tan-ya
the chrysanthemum	*a katalinrózsa*	o kotolinrohzho
cinnamon	*fahéj*	fo-hey
the cucumber	*az ugorka*	oz öögorrko
the currant	*az apró szőlő*	oz oprohserler
the daisy	*a százszorszép*	o sahz-sorrsehp
the dandelion	*a pitypang*	o pity-pong
the elm-tree	*a szilfa*	o silfo
the evergreen	*az örökzöld*	oz ĕrrĕrkzĕrld
the fern	*a páfrány*	o pahfrahny
the fig-tree	*a fügefa*	o feughafo
a filbert	*mogyoró*	mod-yorroh
the fir-tree	*a fenyő*	o fan-yer

English.	Hungarian.	Pronunciation.
a flower	*virág*	virahg
a forest	*erdő*	errder
the fruit-tree	*a gyümölcsfa*	o dyeümĕrlchfo
ginger	*gyömbér*	dyĕrmbehrr
a gooseberry	*egres, piszke*	ag-rash, piska
grape	*szőllő*	serller
horse-chestnut	*vad gesztenye*	vod gas-tan-ya
horse-radish	*torma*	torrmo
the ivy	*a repkény*	o rapkehny
the kernel	*a magbél*	o mogbehl
laurel	*babér*	bobehrr
a leaf	(*fa*) *levél*	(fo) lavehl
a lemon	*citrom*	tsitrom
the lettuce	*a saláta, fejes*	o sholahto, feyash
a lily	*liliom*	liliom
lily-of-the-valley	*gyöngyvirág*	dyĕrndy-virahg
maize	*kukorica*	kŏŏkorritso
maple	*juharfa*	yŏŏ-horrfo
a melon	*dinnye*	dinn-ya
the mistletoe	*a fagyöngy*	o fo-dyĕrndy
a mulberry	*fa-eper*	fo-aperr
the myrtle	*a mirtus*	o mirrtŏŏsh
nettle	*csalán*	cholahn
a nut	*dió*	dioh
the oak (tree)	*a tölgyfa*	o tĕrldy-fo
onion	*hagyma*	hody-mo
orange	*narancs*	norronch
parsnip	*paszternák*	posternahk
peach	*őszibarack*	ersiborrotsk
a pear	*körte*	kĕrr-ta
the peas	*a borsó*	o borrshoh
pepper	*bors*	borrsh
the pine-tree	*a fenyő-fa*	o fan-yer-fo
the pine-apple	*az ananász*	oz ononahss
a pink	*szegfű*	sag-fiu
a plum	*szilva*	silvo
potatoes	*a burgonya*	o bŏŏrgon-yo
primrose	*kankalin*	konkolin
the radish	*a retek*	o rat-ak
raspberry	*málna*	mahlno
the root	*a gyökér*	o dyĕrkehrr

English.	Hungarian.	Pronunciation.
a rose	*rózsa*	rohzho
the spinach	*a paraj*	o porroy
the stalk (of plant)	*a csutka, szár*	o chŏŏtko, sahrr
a strawberry	*szamóca*	somohtso
the stump	*a tönk*	o tĕrnk
tomato	*paradicsom*	porrodichom
a tree	*fa*	fo
trunk	*fatörzs*	fotĕrrzh
a tulip	*tulipán*	toolipahn
turnip	*fehér répa*	fa-hehrr rehpo
vegetables	*zöldség*	zĕrldshehg
the vine	*a szőlőtő*	o serlerter
a violet	*ibolya*	iboyo
a walnut	*dió*	dee-oh
the willow	*a fűzfa*	o fiuzfo

Colours. (*Szinek.*)

(For Shopping see p. 97).

Black	*fekete*	fakata
blue	*kék*	kehk
brown	*barna*	borrno
carmine	*karmin*	korrmin
dark	*sötét*	shĕrteht
green	*zöld*	zĕrld
grey	*szürke*	seurrka
light	*világos*	vilahgosh
orange	*narancssárga*	norronch-shahrgo
purple	*bíborlila*	beeborr-lilo
red	*piros, vörös*	pirrosh, vĕrrĕrsh
violet	*ibolyaszínű*	iboya-seeniu
white	*fehér*	fa-hehr
yellow	*sárga*	shahrrgo

Times, Seasons and Holidays.

(*Idő, évszakok és ünnepek.*)

(For Conversations see p. 105).

The afternoon	*a délután*	o dehlŏŏtahn
the beginning	*a kezdet*	o kazdat
the birthday	*a születésnap*	o siulatehshnop
a century	*évszázad*	ehvsahzod
half-a-century	*félszázad*	fehlsahzod
Christmas	*karácsony*	korrahchony

English.	Hungarian.	Pronunciation.
daily	*napi*	nop-i
dawn, daybreak	*hajnal*	hoynol
the day	*a nap*	o nop
days of the week	*a hét napjai*	o heht nop-yo-i
Sunday	*vasárnap*	voshahrrnop
Monday	*hétfő*	hehtfe*r*
Tuesday	*kedd*	kadd
Wednesday	*szerda*	serrdo
Thursday	*csütörtök*	che͡utě*r*rtě*r*k
Friday	*péntek*	pehntak
Saturday	*szombat*	sombot
the day after to-morrow	*holnapután*	holnopŏŏtahn
the day before yesterday	*tegnapelőtt*	tagnopale*r*tt
to-day, this day	*ma*	mo
Easter	*husvét*	hŏŏshveht
the end	*a vég*	o vehg
the evening	*az este*	oz ashta
a fortnight	*két hét*	keht heht
Good-Friday	*nagypéntek*	nod*y*pehntak
half-an-hour	*fél óra*	fehl ohrro
a holiday	*ünnep*	e͡unnap
Holidays in Hungary	*ünnepek Magyarországban*	e͡unnapak mod-yorr-orrsahgbon
All Saints' day	*mindenszentek napja*	mindensantak nop-yo
Ascension-day	*áldozócsütörtök*	ahldozoh-che͡utě*r*rtě*r*k
Christmas-day	*karácsony*	korrahchon*y*
Easter-day	*husvét vasárnap*	hŏŏshveht voshahrrnop
Good Friday	*nagypéntek*	nod*y*pehntak
New Year's day	*ujév*	ŏŏy-ehv
Mid-Lent	*böjtdereka*	bě*r*yt-darako
an hour	*óra*	ohrro
last month	*a mult hónapban*	o mŏŏlt hohnopbon
last Sunday	*a mult vasárnap*	o mŏŏlt voshahrrnop
last week	*a mult héten*	o mŏŏlt hehtan
leap-year	*a szökő-év*	o sě*r*kě*r*-ehv
Lent	*böjt*	bě*r*yt
Michaelmas	*Szent Mihály napja*	sant mihah-y' nop-yo
midnight	*éjfél*	eh-y'-fehl
the minute	*a perc*	o perrts
a month	*hónap*	hohnop

English.	Hungarian.	Pronunciation.
the months	*a hónapok*	o hohnopok
January	*január*	yonŏŏahrr
February	*február*	fabrŏŏahrr
March	*március*	mahrtsiŏŏsh
April	*április*	ahprilish
May	*május*	mah-yŏŏsh
June	*junius*	yŏŏniŏŏsh
July	*julius*	yŏŏliŏŏsh
August	*augusztus*	owgŏŏstŏŏsh
September	*szeptember*	saptamberr
October	*október*	oktohberr
November	*november*	novamberr
December	*december*	datsamberr
the morning	*a reggel*	o rag-gal
next day	*másnap*	mahshnop
the night	*az éjszaka*	oz eh-y'-soko
noon	*dél*	dehl
a quarter	*negyed*	nad-yad
— of an hour	*negyed óra*	nad-yad ohrro
the seasons	*az évszakok*	oz ehvsokok
spring	*tavasz*	tovoss
summer	*nyár*	nyahrr
autumn	*ősz*	erss
winter	*tél*	tehl
a second	*másodperc*	mahshodperrts
sunrise	*napkelte*	nopkalta
sunset	*napnyugta*	nop-nyŏŏgto
the time	*az idő*	oz ider
to-morrow	*holnap*	holnop
to-night	*ma este*	mo ashta
twilight	*szürkület*	se͡urrke͡ulat
a week	*hét*	heht
this week	*e héten*	e-hehtan
next week	*jövő héten*	yĕrver-hehtan
week-day	*hétköznap*	hehtkĕrznop
weekly	*heti, hetenként*	hat-i, hat-an-kehnt
Whitsuntide	*pünkösd*	pe͡unkĕrshd
a year	*esztendő*	astander
yesterday	*tegnap*	tagnop
— morning	„ *reggel*	„ raggal
— evening	„ *este*	„ ashta

Town and Country. (*Város és falu.*)

(For Conversations see p. 95.)

English.	Hungarian.	Pronunciation.
A bank	*bank*	bonk
the barn	*a csűr*	o chīurr
the bridge	*a híd*	o heed
the brook	*a patak*	o potok
the building	*az épület*	oz ehpe͡ulat
the bush, shrub	*a bokor, cserje*	o bokorr, cherr-ya
the cathedral	*a székesegyház*	o sehkash-edyhahz
the cattle	*a marha*	o morr-ho
a cemetery	*temető*	tam-at-er
the chapel	*a kápolna*	o kahpolno
a chemist	*gyógyszerész*	dyohdy-serrehss
the church	*a templom*	o tamplom
the coffee-room	*a kávézószoba*	o kahvehzohsobo
the country	*az ország, a falu*	oz orrsahg, o folŏŏ
the courtyard	*az udvar*	oz ŏŏdvorr
the custom-house	*a vámház*	o vahmhahz
the dale	*a völgy*	o vĕrldy
a ditch	*árok*	ahrok
the exchange	*a tőzsde*	o terzhda
a farm	*gazdaság*	gozdoshahg
a fence	*palánk*	polahnk
the field	*a mező*	o maz-er
the fisherman	*a halász*	o holahss
the foot-pavement	*a járda*	o yahrrdo
the forest	*az erdő*	oz errder
the gate	*a kapu*	o kopŏŏ
the grass	*a fű*	o fiu
the harbour	*a rév*	o rehv
hay	*széna*	sehno
the herd	*csorda*	chorrdo
the high road	*az országút*	oz orrsahgoot
a hill	*domb*	domb
a hospital	*kórház*	kohrhahz
the hotel	*a szálló*	o sahlloh
the huntsman	*a vadász*	o vodahss
the hut	*a bódé*	o bohdeh
the inn	*a kocsma*	o kotchmo
the log	*a tuskó*	o tŏŏshkoh
the market	*a vásár*	o vahshahrr

English.	Hungarian.	Pronunciation.
the meadow	*a rét*	o reht
a mile	*mértföld*	mehrt-fĕrld
the mill	*a malom*	o molom
a monument	*emlékoszlop*	amlehkoslop
the oats	*a zab*	o zob
the palace	*a palota*	o poloto
a path	*ösvény*	ĕrshvehny
the pier	*a kikötőgát*	o kikĕrtergaht
the police-station	*a rendőrhivatal*	o randerr-hivotol
the post-office	*a postahivatal*	o poshto-hivotol
the prison	*a börtön*	o bĕrrtĕrn
the public-house	*a kocsma*	o kotchmo
the railway-station	*a visúti állomás*	o voshooti ahllomahsh
the river	*a folyó*	o foyoh
the road	*az út*	oz oot
the school	*az iskola*	oz ishkolo
the shepherd	*a juhász*	o yŏŏhahss
a shop	*bolt*	bolt
the soil	*a talaj*	o toloy
a square	*tér*	tehrr
the street	*az utca*	oz ŏŏttso
the telegraph-office	*a távíró-hivatal*	o tahveeroh-hivotol
the theatre	*a színház*	o seenhahz
the timber	*az épületfa*	oz ehpeulatfo
the tower	*a torony*	o torrony
the town	*a város*	o vahrosh
the town-hall	*a város háza*	o vahrosh hahzo
the tramway	*a lóvasút*	o lohvoshoot
the tree	*a fa*	o fo
the university	*az egyetem*	oz ad-yat-am
the valley	*a völgy*	o vĕrldy
the village	*a falu*	o folŏŏ
the waterfall	*a vízesés*	o veezashehsh
the wood	*a hordó*	o horrdoh

Mankind · Relations. (*Emberiség: Rokonsag.*)

The aunt	*a néni*	o nehni
the baby	*a kisbaba, csecsemő*	o kishbobo, chatch-am-[er
a boy	*fiú*	fioo
the bride	*a menyasszony*	o man-yos-sony
the bridegroom	*a vőlegény*	o ver-lag-ehny

English.	Hungarian.	Pronunciation.
the brother	*a fivér*	o fivehrr
the child	*a gyermek*	o dyerrmak
the cousin	*az unokatestvér*	oz öönokotashtvehrr
the cripple	*a nyomorék*	nyomorrehk
the daughter	*a leány*	o le-ahny
— -in-law	*a meny*	o many
the family	*a család*	o cholahd
the father	*az atya*	oz ot-yo
— -in-law	*az ipa, após*	oz ipo, opohsh
a gentleman	*úr*	oor
the girl	*a leány*	o le-ahny
a grandchild	*unoka*	öönoko
the grand-daughter	*az unoka, leány unoka*	oz öönoko, leahny öönoko
the grandfather	*a nagyapa, öregapa*	o nodyopo, ĕrrag-opo
grandmother	*nagyanya, öreganya*	nodyon-yo, ĕrrag-on-yo
the grandson	*az unoka, a fi-unoka*	oz öönoko, o fi-öönoko
the husband	*a férj*	o fehr-y'
a man	*ember*	amberr
a lady	*hölgy*	hĕrldy
the marriage	*a házasság*	o hahzosh-shahg
the mother	*az anya*	oz on-yo
— -in-law	*a napa, az anyós*	o nopo, oz on-yohsh
the nephew	*az unokaöcs*	oz öönoko-ĕrtch
the niece	*az unokahúg*	oz öönoko-hoog
the parents	*a szülők*	o sïulerk
the people	*a nép*	o nehp
person	*személy*	o sameh-y'
single man	*nőtlen ember*	nertlan amberr
single woman	*hajadon*	hoyodon
the sister	*a nővér*	o nervehr
— -in-law	*a sógórnő*	o shohgohrner
the son	*a fiú*	o fioo
the step-father	*a mostoha apa*	o moshto-ho op-o
the step-mother	*a mostoha anya*	o moshto-ho on-yo
the uncle	*a nagybátya*	o nodybaht-yo
the widow	*az özvegyasszony*	oz ĕrzvadyos-sony
the widower	*az özvegyember*	oz ĕrzvadyamberr
the wife	*a feleség*	o falashehg
a woman	*az asszony*	oz ossony
a young lady	*a kisasszony*	o kishossony

The Human Body. (*Az emberi test.*)

English.	Hungarian.	Pronunciation.
The abdomen	*a has*	o hosh
the ankle	*a boka*	o boko
the arm	*a kar*	o korr
the back	*a hát*	o haht
the beard	*a szakáll*	o sokahll
the blood	*a vér*	o vehr
the body	*a test*	o tasht
the bone	*a csont*	o chont
the bowels	*a belek*	o bal-ak
the brain	*az agyvelő*	oz odyval-er
the bust	*a felsőtest*	o falshertasht
the cheek	*az orca*	oz orrtso
the chest	*a mellkas*	o mallkosh
the chin	*az áll*	oz ahll
the complexion	*az arcbőr*	oz orrtsberr
the ear	*a fül*	o fe͡ul
the elbow	*a könyök*	o kĕrn-yĕrk
the eye; the eyes	*a szem*	o sam
the eyebrow	*a szemöldök*	o sam-ĕrl-dĕrk
the eyelid	*a szemhéj*	o sam-heh-y'
the face	*az arc*	oz orrts
the fingers	*az ujj*	oz ŏŏy-y'
the foot	*a láb*	o lahb
the forehead	*a homlok*	o homlok
the hair	*a haj*	o hoy
the hand	*a kéz*	o kehz
the head	*a fej*	o fey
the heart	*a szív*	o seev
the heel	*a sarok*	o shorrok
the kidneys	*a vese*	o vash-a
the knee	*a térd*	o tehrd
the leg	*a lábszár*	o lahbsahr
the limb	*a tag*	o tog
the lip	*az ajak*	oz oyok
the liver	*a máj*	o mah-y'
the lung	*a tüdő*	o te͡uder
the moustache	*a bajusz*	o boyŏŏss
the mouth	*a száj*	o sah-y'
the nail	*a köröm*	o kĕrrĕrm
the neck	*a nyak*	o nyok

English.	Hungarian.	Pronunciation.
the nose	*az orr*	oz orr
the shoulder	*a váll*	o vahll
the side	*az oldal*	oz oldol
the skin	*a bőr*	o běrr
the spine	*a hátgerincz*	o haht-gherrints
the stomach	*a gyomor*	o dyomorr
the temple	*a halánték*	o hol-ahntehk
the teeth	*a fogak, fogazat*	o fogok, fogozot
the throat	*a torok*	o torrok
the thumb	*a hüvelyk*	o hêûveyk
the toe	*a lábújj*	o lahbooy-y'
the tongue	*a nyelv*	o nyalv
the tooth	*a fog*	o fog
the whiskers	*a pofaszakáll*	o pofosokahll
the wrist	*a kézcsukló*	o kehz-chöökloh

Physical and Mental Powers, Qualities, etc.

(*Testi és szellemi erők, tulajdonságok.*)

Age	*kor, életkor*	korr, ehlatkorr
—, old	*öregség*	ěrrag-shehg
anger	*harag*	horrog
art	*művészet*	mïuvehsat
breadth, width	*szélesség*	sehlash-shehg
character	*jellem*	yallam
childhood	*gyermekkor*	dyerrmakkorr
depth	*mélység*	meh-y'-shehg
dislike	*idegenkedés*	idagenkedehsh
emotion	*indulat*	ĭndöölot
fear	*félelem*	fehlalem
foolishness, folly	*bohóság, bolondság*	bohohshahg, bolond-shahg
gentleness	*gyöngédség*	dyěrnghehd-shehg
goodness	*jóság*	yohshahg
greatness	*nagyság*	nodyshahg
hatred	*gyűlölet, gyűlölség*	dyïulěrlat, dyïulěrl-shehg
height	*magasság*	mogosh-shahg
— (stature)	*termet*	terrmat
honesty	*becsületesség*	batch-êûlatash-shehg
dishonesty	*becstelenség*	batch-talanshehg
honour	*becsület*	batch-êûlat
dishonour	*szégyen*	sehdyan
intellect	*értelem*	ehrrtalem

English.	Hungarian.	Pronunciation.
intelligence	*értelmesség, tudósítás*	ehrtalmash-shehg, tŏŏdohsheetahsh
joy	*öröm*	ĕrrĕrm
judgment (faculty)	*ítélet*	eetehlat
knowledge	*tudás*	tŏŏdahsh
laughter, laugh *s.*	*nevetés*	navatehsh
learning	*tanulás*	tonŏŏlahsh
length	*hosszúság*	hossooshahg
love	*szeretet*	seratat
manhood	*férfikor*	fehrfikorr
mind	*értelem, ész*	ehrtalem, ehss
patience	*türelem*	tēūrralem
pleasure	*gyönyör (űség)*	dyĕrn-yĕr (īushehg)
politeness, courtesy	*udvariasság*	ŏŏdvorriosh-shahg
reason (faculty)	*ész, értelem*	ehss, ehrtalem
science	*tudás, tudomány*	tŏŏdahsh, tŏŏdomahny
the senses	*az érzékek*	oz ehrzehkak
feeling, touch	*tapintás*	topintahsh
hearing	*hallás*	hollahsh
seeing, sight	*látás*	lahtahsh
smelling, smell	*szaglás*	soglahsh
tasting, taste	*ízlés*	izlehsh
shape	*alak*	olok
size	*nagyság, méret*	nodyshahg, mehrat
smell (odour)	*szag*	sog
smiling, smile *s.*	*mosoly*	moshoy
sneezing, sneeze *s.*	*tüsszenés*	tēūssanehsh
sorrow	*szomorúság*	somorooshahg
speaking, speech	*beszéd*	bassehd
strength	*erő*	errer
stupidity	*ostobaság*	oshtoboshahg
surprise	*meglepetés*	meglapatehsh
taste (of a thing)	*ízlés*	izlehsh
thickness	*vastagság*	voshtogshahg
thinking, thought	*vélemény* (intrans.), *gondolkozás*	vehlamehny, gondolkozahsh
a thought	*gondolat*	gondolot
voice	*hang*	hong
weakness (quality)	*gyöngeség*	dyĕrn-gashehg
wisdom	*bölcseség*	bĕrlchashehg
youth (quality)	*fiatalság*	fiotolshahg

Health. (*Egészség.*)

(For Conversations see page 95.)

English.	Hungarian.	Pronunciation.
An accident	*baleset*	bolashat
the ambulance	*a mentőkocsi*	o manterkotchi
a bandage	*kötés*	kĕrtehsh
biliousness	*gyomorrontás*	dyomorrontahsh
a bite	*csípés*	cheepehsh
a blister	*hólyag*	hoh-yog
a bruise	*zúzódás*	zoozohdahsh
a burn	*égési seb*	ehg-ehshi shab
contagion	*fertőzés*	ferrterzehsh
a chemist's shop	*gyógyszertár*	dyohdy-serrtahrr
a chill, cold	*meghülés*	meg-heulehsh
—, to catch	*meghűlni*	meg-hiulni
chilblains	*fagy daganat*	fody dogonot
the cough	*a köhögés*	o kĕrhĕrghehsh
the corns	*a tyúkszem*	o tyooksam
cramp	*görcs*	ghĕrrch
the dentist	*a fogorvos*	o fogorrvosh
the diarrhœa	*a hasmenés*	o hoshmanehsh
the diet	*az étrend*	oz ehtrand
the disease, illness	*a betegség*	o bat-ag-shehg
the doctor	*az orvos*	oz orrvosh
the draught	*a korty*	o korty
exercise	*testmozgás*	tashtmozgahsh
exhaustion	*kimerülés*	kimerreulehsh
to faint	*elájulni*	alah-yŏŏlni
fainting	*(el)ájulás*	(al) ah-yŏŏlahsh
the fever	*a láz*	o lahz
the fracture	*a törés*	o tĕrrehsh
the gout	*a köszvény*	o kĕrssvehny
headache	*fejfájás*	feyfah-yahsh
the hospital	*a kórház*	o kohrr-hahz
ill, sick	*beteg*	bat-ag
indigestion	*emésztési zavar (ok)*	amehstehshi zovorr (ok)
indisposition	*rosszullét*	rossŏŏl-leht
inflammation	*gyulladás*	dyŏŏllodahsh
lame	*béna, sánta*	behno, shahnto
the medicine	*az orvosság*	oz orrvosh-shahg
the nurse	*a dajka, az ápolónő*	o doyko. oz ahpolohner

English.	Hungarian.	Pronunciation.
the ointment	*az ír*	oz eer
the pain	*a fájdalom*	o fah-y'-dolom
paralysis	*izombénulás*	izombehnŏŏlahsh
a pill	*pilula*	pilŏŏlo
the poison	*a méreg*	o mehrag
a poultice	*egy meleg borogatás*	edy mal-ag borrogot-ahsh
the prescription	*a recept*	o ratsapt
a rest	*nyugalom*	nyŏŏgolom
a scald	*leforrázás*	laforrahzahsh
a scratch	*karcolás*	korrtsolahsh
the sea-sickness	*a tengeri betegség*	o tangherri batagshehg
sore throat	*torokfájás*	torrokfah-yahsh
a sprain	*ficamodás*	fitsomodahsh
the sting	*a csípés*	o cheepehsh
a tonic	*az erősitő*	errershеeter
the wound	*a seb*	o shab

Food & Drink. (*Etel és ital.*)

(For Shopping see p. 97.)

The bread	*a kenyér*	o kenyehrr
—, brown	*a fekete kenyér*	o fakata kenyehrr
—, new	*az új kenyér*	oz ooy kenyehrr
—, stale	*a száraz kenyér*	o sahroz kenyehrr
beverage, drink	*ital*	itol
beer	*sör*	shĕrr
chocolate	*csokoládé*	chokolahdeh
coffee	*kávé*	kahveh
lemonade	*citromosvíz*	tsitromoshveez
milk	*tej*	tey
soda water	*szódavíz*	sohdoveez
tea	*tea*	te-o
water	*víz*	veez
wine	*bor*	borr
the breakfast	*a reggeli*	o raggali
the butter	*a vaj*	o voy
a cake	*kalács, sütemény*	kolahch, sheutamehny
cheese	*sa*	shoyt
the chicken	*a csirke*	o chirr-ka
cream	*tejszín*	teyseen
the dinner	*az ebéd*	oz ab-ehd
egg	*tojás*	toyahsh

English.	Hungarian.	Pronunciation.
the flour	*a liszt*	o list
hunger	*éhség*	eh-shehg
meat	*hús*	hoosh
—, boiled	*főtt hús*	fertt hoosh
—, roast	*sült hús*	sheult hoosh
bacon	*szalonna*	solonno
beef	*marhahús*	morr-ho-hoosh
beefsteak	*marha szelet*	morr-ho sal-at
fat	*zsir*	zhirr
ham	*sonka*	shonko
kidneys	*vesék*	vasha
lamb	*bárány*	bahrahny
lean	*sovány*	shovahny
mutton	*ürűhús*	eurïuhoosh
pork	*disznóhús*	dissnoh-hoosh
a sausage	*kolbász*	kolbahss
veal	*borjúhús*	borr-yoo-hoosh
mustard	*mustár*	mŏŏshtahrr
oil	*olaj*	oloy
an omelet	*tojáslepény*	toyahsh-lap-ehny
pepper	*bors*	borrsh
a pudding	*pudding, tésztásétel*	pŏŏdding, tehstahsh-ehtal
rice	*rizs*	rizh
the roll	*a zsemle*	o zhamla
salad	*saláta*	sholahto
salt	*só*	shoh
smoking	*dohányzás*	do-hahnyzahsh
a cigar	*szivar*	sivorr
cigarette	*cigaretta*	tsigoretto
matches	*gyufa*	dyŏŏfo
pipe	*pipa*	pipo
the tobacco	*a dohány*	o do-hahny
the soup	*a leves*	o lavash
sugar	*cukor*	tsŏŏkorr
the supper	*a vacsora*	o votchorro
thirst	*szomjuság*	som-yŏŏ-shahg
toothpick	*fog-piszkáló*	fog-piskahloh
under-done	*félnyers*	fehl-nyersh
vegetables	*zöldség*	zĕrld-shehg
vinegar	*ecet*	atsat
well-done	*jól átsült*	yohl ahtsheult

Cooking & Eating Utensils. (*Főző és evő eszközök.*)

(For Shopping see p. 97.)

English.	Hungarian.	Pronunciation.
A basin	*medence*	madantsa
a coffee-pot	*kávéskanna*	kahvehsh-konno
a corkscrew	*dugóhúzó*	dŏŏgoh-hoozoh
the cruet-stand	*az ecet-olajtar*	oz atsat-oloytorrtoh
a cup	*csésze*	cheh-sa
the decanter	*a palack*	o polotsk
the dish	*a tál*	o tahl
a fork	*villa*	villo
a frying-pan	*serpenyő*	sherrpan-yer
a glass	*pohár*	pohahrr
a grill	*sütőrács*	sheuterrahch
a kettle	*üst*	eusht
a knife	*kés*	kehsh
the nut-crackers	*a diótörő*	o dioh-tĕrrer
an oven	*sütő*	sheuter
the plate	*a tányér*	o tahn-yehrr
the salt-cellar	*a sótartó*	o shohtorrtoh
a saucepan	*lábas*	lahbosh
a saucer	*csészealja*	cheh-sa-ol-yo
the serviette	*az asztalkendő*	oz ostolkander
the soup-ladle	*a levesmerő*	o lavashmerrer
a spoon	*kanál*	konahl
a stove	*kályha, tűzhely*	kah-y'-ho, tiuz-hey
the table-cloth	*az asztalterítő*	oz ostoltereeter
the tea-pot	*a teáskanna*	o ta-ahsh-konno
a tray	*tálca*	tahltso
the water-bottle	*a vizes palack*	o vizash polotsk
a wine-glass	*boros pohár*	borrosh pohahrr

Dress & the Toilet. (*Ruházat és öltözködés.*)

(For Shopping see p. 97; Dressmaker, p. 98.)

English.	Hungarian.	Pronunciation.
Bath	*fürdő*	feurrder
bodice	*ruhaderék*	rŏŏhoderrehk
the bonnet	*a fejkötő, a női kalap*	o feykĕrter, o neri kolop
the boot	*a cipő, csizma*	o tsiper, chizmo
the bootjack	*a cipőhúzó*	o tsiper-hoozoh
the bootlaces	*a cipőkötő*	o tsiper-kĕrter
bow	*csokor*	chokorr
the bracelet	*a karperecz*	o korrperrats

English.	Hungarian.	Pronunciation.
the braces	*a nadrágtartó*	o nodrahg-torrtoh
the breeches	*a nadrág*	o nodrahg
the brush	*a kefe*	o ka-fa
—, clothes-	*a ruhakefe*	o rŏŏhokafa
—, nail-	*a körömkefe*	o kĕrrĕrmkafa
—, tooth-	*a fogkefe*	o fogkafa
the brooch	*a melltű*	o malltīu
the buckle	*a csat*	o chot
the button	*a gomb*	o gomb
the button-hook	*a cipő gomboló*	o tsiper gomboloh
the cap	*a sipka*	o shipko
a cloak	*felöltő*	falĕrlter
clothing, dress	*ruházat, ruha*	rŏŏhahzot, rŏŏho
a coat	*kabát*	kobaht
the collar	*a gallér*	o gollehrr
the comb	*a fésü*	o fehsheu
corset, stays	*füző*	fiuzer
the cotton	*a gyapot*	o dyopot
drawers	*lábravaló*	lahbrovoloh
the dress	*a ruha*	o rŏŏho
the garters	*a harisnyakötő*	o horrish-nyokĕrter
the gloves	*a kesztyű*	o kastyīu
the hairpin	*a hajtű*	o hoytīu
a handkerchief	*zsebkendő*	zhabkander
the hat	*a kalap*	o kolop
the hat-pin	— *tű*	o kolop tīu
the mackintosh	*az esőköpeny*	oz asherkĕrpany
muff	*karmantyú*	korrmont-yoo
a needle	*varrótű*	vorrohtīu
an overcoat	*felső kabát, felöltő*	falsher kobaht, falĕrlter
the parasol	*a napernyő*	o noperrn-yer
the petticoat	*az alsó szoknya*	oz olshoh soknyo
the pin	*a gombostű*	o gomboshtīu
the pocket	*a zseb*	o zhab
the purse	*a pénztárca*	o pehnztahrtso
the razor	*a borotva*	o borrotvo
a ring	*gyűrü*	dyīurreu
scissors	*az olló*	oz olloh
a shirt	*ing*	ing
sewing-cotton	*a cérna*	o tsehrrno
the shoe-horn	*a cipőhúzó*	o tsiper-hoozoh

English.	Hungarian.	Pronunciation.
the shoe	*a cipő*	o tsiper
the skirt	*a ruhaalj*	o rŏŏ-ho-ol-y'
the sleeve	*az ujj*	oz ŏŏy-y'
the slippers	*a papucs*	o popŏŏch
the soap	*a szappan*	o soppon
the spectacles	*a szemüveg*	o sameuvag
the stockings	*a harisnya*	o horrishnyo
the thread	*a fonal, szál*	o fonol, sahl
the tie, neck-tie	*a nyakkendő*	o nyokkander
the tooth-powder	*a fogpor*	o fogporr
the trousers	*a nadrág*	o nodrahg
the umbrella	*az ernyő*	oz errn-yer
the veil	*a fátyol*	o faht-yol
the waistcoat	*a mellény*	o mallehny
a watch	*zsebóra*	zhabohrro

Washing List. (*Mosó-jegyzék.*)

(For Laundress see p. 99.)

Aprons	*kötény*	kĕrtehny
blankets	*gyapjúpokróc*	dyop-yoo-pokrohts
blouses	*blúz, zubbony*	blooz, zŏŏbbony
bodices	*derék*	derrehk
caps	*fejkötő*	feykĕrter
chemises	*női ing*	neri ing
collars, lace	*gallérok, csipke*	gollehrok, chipka
—, linen	*vászon gallérok*	vahson gollehrok
combinations	*alsó öltözet*	olshoh ĕrltĕrzat
cuffs	*kézelők*	kehzelerk
drawers	*lábravaló*	lahbrovoloh
dresses	*ruha*	rŏŏho
dressing-gowns	*hálóköntös*	hahlohkĕrntĕrsh
handkerchiefs, [pocket-	*zsebkendők*	zhabkanderk
—, silk	*selyem zsebkendők*	sheyam zhabkanderk
napkins	*asztalkendők*	ostolkanderk
neckties	*nyakkendők*	nyokkanderk
night-shirts, dress-[es	*háló ingek*	hahlo ingak
pants (drawers)	*alsó nadrág*	olshoh nodrahg
petticoats, flannel	*flanel alsó szoknya*	flonel olshoh soknyo
pillow-cases	*vánkoshéjak*	vahnkosh-heh-yok
pinafores	*kötény*	kertehny
pyjamas (suits)	*alsó nadrágok*	olshoh nodrahgok

English.	Hungarian.	Pronunciation.
serviettes	*asztalkendők*	ostolkanderk
sheets	*lepedő*	lapader
shirts	*ingek*	ingak
sleeves	*ujjak* [*ca*	ŏŏy-yok [tso
socks	*férfi harisnya, kap-*	fehrfi horrishnyo, kop-
stockings	*női harisnya*	neri horrishnyo
—, silk	*selyem harisnya*	sheyam horrishnyo
table-cloths	*asztalterítő, abrosz*	ostolterriter, obross
towels	*törülközők*	těrreŭlkěrzerk
under-vests	*alsó-ing*	olshoh-ing
waistcoat, flannel	*flanel mellény*	flonel mallehny

House and Furniture. (*Ház és butorzat.*)

(For Shopping see p. 97.)

The ante-room	*az előszoba*	oz alersobo
an armchair	*karszék*	korrsehk
the ashes	*a hamu*	o homŏŏ
the attic	*a padlásszoba*	o podlahsh-sobo
the basin	*a medence*	o madantsa
the bathroom	*a fürdőszoba*	o feŭrdersobo
the bed, bedstead	*az ágy*	oz ahdy
the bedroom	*a hálószoba*	o hahlohsobo
the bell	*a csengő*	o chan-gher
the blanket	*a gyapjúpokrócz*	o dyop-yoo-pokrohts
the blind	*az ablakredőny*	oz oblokraderny
the bolt	*a tolózár*	o tolohzahrr
the book	*a könyv*	o kěrnyv
— -case	*a könvyszekrény*	o kěrnyv-sakrehny
— -shelf	*a könyvespolc*	o kěrnyvashpolts
a box	*doboz, láda*	doboz, lahdo
a bracket	*polc, állvány*	polts, ahlvahny
the brick	*a tégla*	o tehglo
a broom	*seprő*	shaprer
the candle	*a gyertya*	o dyerrt-yo
the candlestick	*a gyertya-tartó*	o dyerrt-yo-torrtoh
the carpet	*a szőnyeg*	o sernyag
the ceiling	*a mennyezet*	o menn-yazat
the cellar	*a vince*	o pintsa
a chair	*szék*	sehk
the coals	*a kőszén*	o kersehn
the counterpane	*az ágyterítő*	oz ahdyterreeter

English.	Hungarian.	Pronunciation.
a cupboard	*polcosszekrény*	poltsosh-sakrehny
the curtain	*a függöny*	o fe͡ugğĕrny
a cushion	*párna, vánkos*	pahrrno, vahnkosh
the dining-room	*az ebédlő*	oz abehdler
the drawing-room	*a szalon, társalgó*	o solon, tahrrsholgoh
a feather bed	*derékalj*	derrehkol-y'
the flame	*a láng*	o lahng
the floor (storey)	*az emelet*	oz am-al-at
a foot-stool	*zsámoly*	zhahmoy
furniture, piece of	*bútor*	bootorr
the garden	*a kert*	o kerrt
the house	*a ház*	o hahz
the iron	*a vas*	o vosh
the key	*a kulcs*	o kŏŏlch
the kitchen	*a konyha*	kony-ho
the lamp	*a lámpa*	o lahmpo
a lid	*fedő*	fad-er
the lock	*a lakat*	o lok-ot
a looking-glass	*tükör*	te͡ukĕrr
the matches	*a gyufa*	o dyŏŏfo
the mattress	*a matrac*	o motrots
a picture	*kép*	kehp
a pillow	*vánkos*	vahnkosh
a pillow-case	*vánkoshéj*	vahnkosh-heh-y'
the poker	*a tűzkaparó*	o tiuzkoporoh
a pot	*edény*	ad-ehny
the roof	*a tető*	o tat-er
the room	*a szoba*	o sob-o
a seat	*ülés*	e͡ulehsh
the sheet	*a lepedő*	o lap-ad-er
the shovel	*a lapát*	o lopaht
the sideboard	*a pohárszék*	o pohahrrsehk
the smoke	*a füst*	o fe͡usht
the soot	*a korom*	o korrom
a spark	*szikra*	sikro
the staircase	*a lépcsőház*	o lehpcherhahz
the stairs	*a lépcső*	o lehpcher
the stone	*a kő*	o ker
a table	*asztal*	ostol
a trunk	*bőrönd*	berrĕrnd
the vase	*a virágtartó*	o virahg-torrtoh

English.	Hungarian.	Pronunciation.
the wall	*a fal*	o fol
— -paper	*a falkárpit*	o fol-kahrrpit
a wax-candle	*viasz gyertya*	vioss dyerrt-yo
the window	*az ablak*	oz oblok
the wood	*a tüzelőfa*	o teũzalerfo
a writing-desk	*íróasztal*	eeroh-ostol

Travelling. (*Utazás.*)

(For Conversations see pp 88—91.)

The arrival	*a megérkezés*	o megehrrkazehsh
the bill	*a számla*	o sahmlo
the box	*a doboz, bőrönd*	o doboz, berrĕrnd
the bridle	*a kantár*	o kontahrr
a cabman	*kocsis*	kotchish
a carriage	*kocsi*	kotchi
the cloak-room	*a ruhatár*	o rŏŏhotahrr
the coach	*a kocsi*	o kotchi
a cushion	*párna*	pahrrno
a custom-house [officer	*vám hivatalnok*	vahm hivotolnok
the departure	*az elutazás*	oz alŏŏtozahsh
the engine	*a gőzgép*	o gherz-ghehp
first-class ticket	*első-osztályú jegy*	alsher-ostah-yoo yady
foot-warmer	*láb melegítő*	lahb mal-ag-eeter
the guard	*az őr*	oz err
a guide	*vezető*	vaz-at-er
a guide-book	*vezérkönyv*	vazehrrkĕrnyv
a hat-box	*kalapdoboz*	kolopdoboz
the hotel	*a szálloda*	o sahllodo
the interpreter	*a tolmács*	o tolmahch
the key	*a kulcs*	o kŏŏlch
the landlady	*a háziasszony*	o hahziossony
the landlord	*a háziúr*	o hahzioorr
the luggage	*a podgyász*	o pod-dyahss
the office	*a hivatal*	o hivotol
an omnibus	*társaskocsi*	tahrrshosh-kotchi
the payment	*a fizetés*	o fizatehsh
the porter	*a hordár*	o horrdahrr
the railway	*a vaspálya*	o voshpah-yo
— -carriage	*a vasuti kocsi*	o voshŏŏti kotchi
— -station	*a vasuti állomás*	o voshŏŏti ahllomahsh
a receipt	*elismervény*	alishmerrvehny

English.	Hungarian.	Pronunciation.
the reins	*a kantárszár*	o kontahrrsahrr
the road	*az út*	oz oot
the rug	*a pokróc*	o pokrohts
a saddle	*nyereg*	nyerreg
the station-master	*az állomás főnök*	oz ahllomahsh fernĕrk
a strap	*szíj*	see-y'
the ticket	*a jegy*	o yady
— -office	*a jegypénztár*	o yady-pehnztahrr
the train	*a vonat*	o von-ot
the trunk	*az utiláda*	oz ŏŏtilahdo
the voyage	*az utazás*	oz ŏŏtozahsh
the waiter	*a pincér*	o pin-tsehrr
the waiting-room	*a váróterem*	o vahrohterrem

Travelling by Ship. (*Utazás : a gőzhajón.*)

(For Conversations see p. 90.)

Alongside, to come	*mellé jönni*	malleh yĕrnni
anchor	*horgony*	horrgony
berth	*hajószoba*	hoyohsobo
boat	*hajó*	hoyoh
boiler	*kazán*	kozahn
bow	*(hajó)homlok*	(hoyoh) homlok
buoy	*bója*	boh-yo
cabin	*hajókamra*	hoyoh-komro
cable	*hajókötél*	hoyoh-kĕrtehl
captain	*kapitány*	kopitahny
compass	*iránytű*	irrahnytüu
crane	*emelő darú*	am-al-er dorroo
crew	*(hajó)legénység*	(hoyoh) lag-ehny-shehg
deck	*födélzet*	fĕrdehlzat
to disembark, *trans.*	*kiszállítni (hajón)*	kisahlleetni (hoyohn)
—, *intr.*	*kiszállni*	kisahllni
dock	*raktárudvar*	roktahrŏŏdvorr
to embark, *trans.*	*hajóra rakni*	hoyohro rokni
—, *intr.*	*hajóra szállni*	hoyohro sahllni
engineer	*mérnök*	mehrrnĕrk
fishing-boat	*halászbárka*	holahss-bahrrko
flag	*lobogó*	lobogoh
gangway	*kikötőhid*	kikĕrterhid
harbour, port	*kikötő*	kikĕrter
helm, rudder	*kormány (hajóé)*	korrmahny (hoyoh-eh)

English.	Hungarian.	Pronunciation.
hold	*fogás*	fogahsh
to land	*kirak (hajóból), kikötni, kirakodni*	kirrok (hoyohbohl), kikĕrtni, kirrokodni
landing-stage, pier	*kikötőgát*	kikĕrtergaht
life-belt	*mentő-öv*	manter-ĕrv
life-boat	*mentő-csónak*	manter-chohnok
lighthouse	*világító-torony*	vilahgheetoh-torrony
mast	*árbocz*	ahrrbots
oar	*evező (lapát)*	av-az-er (lopaht)
paddle-wheel	*(hajó)kerék*	(hoyoh) kerrehk
passenger	*utazó*	ŏŏtozoh
pilot	*kormányos*	korrmahn-yosh
port-hole	*nyílás*	nyeelahsh
quay	*kőpart*	kerporrt
rope	*kötél*	kĕrtehl
sailing-ship	*hajó(vitorlás)*	hoyoh (vitorrlahsh)
saloon (1st class)	*(hajón)díszterem, első osztály*	(hoyohn) deesterrem, alsher ostah-y'
screw-propeller	*csavargőzös*	chovorrgherzĕrsh
seaman, sailor	*hajós*	hoyohsh
ship	*hajó* [intr.	hoyoh
to start	*felhajt*, trans., *indul*,	falhoyt. indŏŏl
steam-boat, -ship	*gőzhajó*	gherz-hoyoh
steerage, 3rd class	*harmadosztályú*	horrmodostah-yoo
steersman	*kormányos*	korrmahn-yosh
stern	*hajófar*	hoyohforr
steward	*(hajón) élelmező-mester* (*jón*)	(hoyohn) ehlalmazer-mashterr [yohn)
stewardess	*(nő)kiszolgáló* (*ha-*	(ner) kisolgahloh (ho-
tug	*vontatóhajó*	vontotoh-hoyoh
voyage	*utazás*	ŏŏtozahsh

Countries and Nations. (*Országok és nemzetek.*)

Africa	*Afrika*	ofriko
America	*Amerika*	omeriko
an American	*amerikai*	omeriko-i
Asia	*Ázsia*	ahzhio
Austria	*Ausztria*	owstrio
a Belgian	*belga*	belgo
Belgium	*Belgium*	belghiŏŏm
a country	*ország*	orrsahg

English.	Hungarian.	Pronunciation.
Cuba	*Kuba*	kŏŏbo
a Dane	*dán*	dahn
Denmark	*Dánia*	dahnio
a Dutchman	*hollandi*	hollondi
the empire	*a császárság*	o chahsahrrshahg
England	*Anglia*	onglio
an Englishman	*angol*	ongol
Europe	*Európa*	e-ŏŏrohpo
France	*Franciaország*	frontsio-orrsahg
a Frenchman	*francia*	frontsio
a German	*német (ember)**	nehmat (amberr)
Germany	*Németország*	nehmatorrsahg
Holland	*Hollandia*	hollondio
a Hungarian	*magyar (ember)*	mod-yorr (amberr)
Hungary	*Magyarország*	mod-yorr-orrsahg
Ireland	*Irország*	irrorrsahg
an Irishman	*ír*	eerr
an Italian	*olasz (ember)*	oloss (amberr)
Italy	*Olaszország*	olossorrsahg
the kingdom	*a királyság*	o kirah-y'-shahg
a republic	*a köztársaság*	o kerztahrr-shoshahg
Russia	*Oroszország*	orossorrsahg
a Russian	*orosz (ember)*	oross (amberr)
a Scotchman	*skót*	shkoht
Scotland	*Skótország*	shkohtorrsahg
Spain	*Spanyolország*	shpon-yol-orrsahg
a Spaniard	*spanyol (ember)*	shpon-yol (amberr)
a Swede	*svéd (ember)*	shvehd (amberr)
Sweden	*Svédország*	shvehdorrsahg
a Swiss	*svájci (ember)*	shveyt-si (amberr)
Switzerland	*Svájc*	shveyts

Amusements. (*Szórakozások.*)

(For Conversations see p. 100.)

A ball	*bál*	bahl
the carnival	*a farsang*	o forrshong
a circus	*cirkusz*	tsirrkŏŏss
a concert	*hangverseny*	hong-verrshany
the accompanist	*a kisérő*	o kishehrer
the accompaniment	*a kiséret*	o kishehrat
the band	*a zenekar*	o zan-a-korr

* "Ember" signifies *man;* it may be omitted. See p. 84, para. 3.

English.	Hungarian.	Pronunciation.
the chorus	*az énekkar*	oz ehnakkorr
the conductor	*a karmester*	o korrmashterr
the drum	*a dob*	o dob
a duet	*kettős*	kattersh
the instruments	*a hangszer*	o hong-serr
—, brass	*a réz hangszer*	o rehz hong-serr
—, string	*a húros hangszer*	o hoorosh hong-serr
the music	*a zene*	o zan-a
the orchestra	*a zenekar*	o zanakorr
the organ	*az orgona*	oz orrgono
a part-song	*kar ének*	korr ehnak
the pianist	*a zongorás*	o zongorrahsh
the piano	*a zongora*	o zongorro
the programme	*a műsor*	o mīushorr
to play (music)	*játszani*	yahtsoni
the recital	*az előadás*	oz al-erodahsh
a recitation	*szavalat*	sovolot
a singer	*énekes*	ehnakash
a solo	*magánének*	mogahnehnak
a song	*ének, dal*	ehnak, dol
a trumpet	*trombita*	trombito
a violin	*hegedű*	hag-ad-īu
the exhibition	*a kiállitás*	o kiahllitahsh
the fête	*a mulatság, az ünnep*	o mŏŏlotshahg, oz ēūnnap
the flower-show	*a virág-kiállitás*	o virahg-kiahllitahsh
the museum	*a múzeum*	o moozeŏŏm
the music-hall	*az orfeum, a dalcsarnok*	oz orrfeŏŏm, o dolchorrnok
the opera	*az opera*	oz opero
the opera-glasses	*a színházi látcső*	o seenhahzi laht-cher
the opera-house	*az operaház*	oz operohahz
picture gallery	*képtár*	kehptahrr
sports and games	*testedzés és játékok*	tashtadzehsh ehsh yahtehkok
billiards	*billiárd*	billiahrd
boxing	*ökölvívás*	ĕrkĕrlveevahsh
chess	*sakk*	shokk
draughts	*ostábla*	oshtahblo
golf	*golf*	golf
the grand-stand	*a főemelvény*	o fer-amalvehny
the jockey	*a versenylovas*	o verrshany-lovosh
the match	*a játszma, küzdelem*	o yahtsmo, kēūzdalem

English.	Hungarian.	Pronunciation.
sports, *contd.*		
to play (a game)	*játszani*	yahtsoni
polo	*lovaslabda*	lovoshlobdo
the races	*a verseny*	o verrshan*y*
the race-course	*a lóversenytér*	o lohverrshan*y*-tehrr
the regatta	*a csónakverseny*	o chohnokverrshan*y*
tennis	*tennisz, hálóslabda*	tennis, hahlohsh-lobdo
the theatre	*a színház*	o seenhahz
the act	*a felvonás*	o falvonahsh
the actor	*a színész*	o seenehss
the actress	*a színésznő* [*nő* f.	o seenehssne*r* [ne*r*
the artist	*a művész* m., *művész-*	o mïuvehss, mïuvehss-
the auditorium	*a nézőtér*	o nehze*r*tehrr
the ballet	*a ballett*	o bollett
the box-office	*a jegy-pénztár*	o yad*y*-pehnztahrr
the cloak-room	*a ruhatár*	o rŏŏhotahrr
the comedian	*a színész*	o seenehss
the comedy	*a vígjáték*	o veeg-yahtehk
the curtain	*a függöny*	o feug-ghĕrn*y*
the dancer, *f.*	*a táncos (nő)*	o tahntsosh (ne*r*)
the exit	*a kijárás*	o ki-yahrrahsh
the footlights	*a színpadi lámpák*	o seenpodi lahmpahk
the play	*a színdarab*	o seendorrob
the programme	*a színlap*	o seenlop
the proprietor	*a tulajdonos*	o tŏŏloydonosh
the refreshment-	*az étterem*	oz ehtterrem
the scene [room	*a színpad*	o seenpod
the seats	*az ülések*	oz eulehshek
the boxes	*a páholyok*	o pah-hoyok
the gallery	*a karzat*	o korrzot
the pit	*a földszint*	o feuldsint
reserved seats	*fenntartott helyek*	fanntorrtott heyak
the stalls	*a támlásszékek*	o tahmlash-sehkak
the stage	*a színpad*	o seenpod
— -manager	*a rendező*	o rendeze*r*
the ticket	*a jegy*	o yad*y*
the tragedian	*a tragikus színész*	o trog-ikŏŏsh seenehss
the tragedy	*a szomorújáték*	o somorroo-yahtehk

Cycling. (*Kerékpár.*)

(For Conversations see page 101.)

English.	Hungarian.	Pronunciation.
Accessories	*kellékek*	kallehkak
axle ; front, back	*tengely ; homlok, hát*	tang-ey ; homlok, haht
backbone	*gerincz*	gherrints
ball bearings	*tengely golyók*	tangey goyohk
bell	*csengő*	chang-er
bicycle	*kerékpár*	kerrehkpahrr
bolt (screw-)	*csavar*	chovorr
brake	*kerékkötő*	kerrehk-kĕrter
cement	*cement*	tsamant
chain	*lánc*	lahnts
chainless	*láncnélküli*	lahnts-nehlkeu͡li
chain-regulator	*lánc szabályozó*	lahnts sobah-yozoh
— -wheel	*lánc kerék*	lahnts kerrehk
cone ; front, back	*kúp ; homlok, hátsó*	koop; homlok, halt-shoh
connection	*összekötés*	ĕrssakĕrtehsh
crank	*pedáltengely*	pedahl-tangey
— -pin	*pedáltengely tű*	pedahl-tangey tüu
crooked	*görbe*	ghĕrrba
crossbar	*kereszt rúd*	kerrast rood
cyclist	*kerékpáros*	kerrehkpahrosh
cycling race	*kerékpár verseny*	kerrehkpahrr verrshany
cyclometer	*kerékpár óra*	kerrehkpahrr ohrro
to dismount	*leszállni*	lassahllni
to electro-plate	*ezüstözni*	azeu͡shtĕrzni
to enamel	*zománcozni*	zomahntsozni
footstep	*lábnyom*	lahb-nyom
fork	*villa*	villo
frame	*váz, szerkezet*	vahz, serrkazat
friction	*horzsolódás*	horr-zholohdahsh
gear	*az áttétel*	oz ahttehtal
—, high	*nagy áttétel*	nody ahttehtal
—, low	*kis áttétel*	kish ahttehtal
gear-case	*áttétel-tok*	ahttehtal-tok
handle, grips	*fogantyú*	fogont-yoo
handle-bar	*kormányrúd*	korrmahny-rood
hub	*agy*	ody
indiarubber	*gummi*	gŏŏmmi
— solution	*gummi oldat*	gŏŏmmi oldot
knapsack	*utitáska, utizsák*	ŏŏtitahshko, ŏŏti-zhahk

English.	Hungarian.	Pronunciation.
lamp	*lámpa*	lahmpo
— -bracket	*lámpalécz*	lahmpo-lehts
— -wick	*lámpabél*	lahmpo-behl
to light up	*lámpát gyujtani*	lahmpaht dyŏŏytoni
lubricator	*olajozó*	oloy-ozoh
— protector	*olajtartó-védő*	oloytorrtoh-vehder
luggage-carrier	*podgyász-tartó*	poddyahss-torrtoh
map	*térkép*	tehrrkehp
to mount	*felszállni*	falsahllni
mudguard	*sárellenző*	shahrallanzer
nut	*csavarzár*	chovorrzahrr
—, safety	*biztonsági csavarzár*	biztonshahgi chovorr-
oil for burning	*lámpa olaj*	lahmpo oloy [zahrr
— for lubricating	*olajozó*	oloyozoh
oil-can	*olajkanna*	oloykonno
pedal	*lábító, pedál*	lahbeetoh, pedahl
— -rubber	*lábító-, pedál-gummi*	lahbeetoh-, pedahl-
pump	*szivattyú*	sivott-yoo [gŏŏmmi
— -tube	*szivattyúcső*	sivott-yoo-cher
to pump	*felfujtatni*	falfŏŏytotni
rags, some	*rongyok*	rond-yok
repairing outfit	*javitó felszerelés*	yovitoh falserralehsh
rim	*kerékabroncs*	kerrehkobronch
saddle	*nyereg*	nyerrag
— -bag	*nyereg zsák (iszák)*	nyerrag zhahk (issahk)
— -pillar	*nyeregnyél*	nyerrag-nyehl
screw	*csavar*	chovorr
— -bolt of chain	*lánczár*	lahntszahrr
— -driver	*csavarhajtó*	chovorr-hoytoh
to screw	*csavarni*	chovorrni
spanner	*kulcs, csavarforgató*	kŏŏlch, chovorrforr-
spokes	*küllők*	keüllerk [gotoh
spring	*rugó*	rŏŏgoh
to start	*indulni*	indŏŏlni
to steer	*vezetni*	vazatni
strap	*szíj*	see-y'
to take to pieces	*szétszedni*	sehtsadni
to tighten up	*szoritani*	sorritoni
toe clip	*lábújj fogó*	lahbooy-y' fogoh
tricycle	*hármaskerék*	hahrmoshkerrehk
trousers clip	*nadrág csat*	nodrahg chot

English.	Hungarian.	Pronunciation.
tube, inner	*belső cső*	balsher cher
—, outer cover	*külső cső*	ke͡ulsher cher
tyre, hollow	*üreges abroncs*	e͡uragash obronch
—, pneumatic	*gummi abroncs*	gŏŏmmi obronch
—, solid	*tömörabroncs*	tĕrmĕrrobronch
to unscrew	*lecsavarni*	latchovorrni
valve	*szelep*	salap
wallet	*bőrtáska*	berrtahshka
wheel, front	*homlok kerék*	homlok kerrehk
—, back	*hátsó kerék*	hahtshoh kerrehk
wheels	*kerekek*	kerrakak

Photography. (*Fényképezés.*)

(For Conversations see page 102.)

English.	Hungarian.	Pronunciation.
Background	*háttér*	hahtte͡urr
— cloth	*háttér vászon*	hahttehrr vahson
camera	*fényképező gép*	fehnykehpazer ghehp
dark-room lamp	*sötét kamra lámpa*	sĕrteht komro lahmpo
dark slide (double)	*lemezvédő*	lamaz-vehder
developing	*előhivás*	alerhivahsh
dipper	*fürdő*	fe͡urrder
dishes	*tálak*	tahlok
dish for developing	*előhivó tál*	alerhivoh tahl
— for fixing	*rögzítő tál*	rĕrgzeeter tahl
— for toning	*színező tál*	seenazer tahl
draining-rack	*szárító rács*	sahrreetoh rahch
dry plates	*száraz lemezek*	sahrroz lamazek
films	*lemezek*	lamazek
flash-lamp	*magnézium lámpa*	mognehziŏŏm lahmpo
focussing glass	*beállító üveg*	ba-ahlleetoh e͡uvag
funnel	*tölcsér*	terl-chehr
glass measure	*mérő üveg*	mehrrer e͡uvag
iris diaphragm	*iris diafragma*	irrish diofrogmo
lens	*lencse*	lan-cha
—, cap of	*lencsefedő*	lanchafader
plate-holder	*lemeztartó*	lamaztorrtoh
— -lifter	*lemez fogó*	lamaz fogoh
platinotypes	*platinotipia*	plotinotipio
printing	*másolás*	mahsholahsh
— frame	*másoló keret*	mahsholoh ka-rat
scales and weights	*mérleg és sulyok*	mehrrlag ehsh shŏŏ-yok

English.	Hungarian.	Pronunciation.
shutter	*csapó*	chopoh
—, instantaneous	*azonnali*	ozonnoli
speed indicator	*időmutató*	idermŏŏtotoh
squeegee	*kaucsuk henger*	ko-ŏŏ-chŏŏk hangerr
tripod (twofold)	*háromláb*	hahromlahb
view-finders	*tárgykeresők*	tahrrdy-ka-rasherk
—, square	*négyzetes* —	nehdyzatesh
—, oblong	*hosszukás* —	hossŏŏkahsh
washing tanks	*öblitő*	ĕrbliter

Religion. (*Vallás.*)

(For Conversations see p. 103.)

English.	Hungarian.	Pronunciation.
Absolution	*feloldozás*	faloldozahsh
the altar	*az oltár*	oz oltahrr
the baptism	*a keresztelés*	o ka-rast-alehsh
the cardinal	*a bibornok*	o biborrnok
the cathedral	*a székesegyház*	o sehkashedyhahz
the chapel	*a kápolna*	o kahpolno
the choir (place)	*a templom karzat*	o tamplom korrzot
— (singers)	*énekkar*	ehnakkorr
the church	*a templom*	o tamplom
the Communion	*a gyónás*	o dyohnahsh
the convent	*a kolostor*	o koloshtorr
a fast-day	*böjt nap*	beryt nop
a festival	*ünnep*	ĕŭnnap
the font	*a keresztelőmedence*	o karastalermadantsa
the lectern	*a pulpitus*	o pŏŏlpitŏŏsh
the litany	*a litánia*	o litahnio
mass, high	*nagymise*	nodymish-a
—, low	*kismise*	kishmish-a
matins	*reggeli istentisztelet*	rag-gali ishtantistalat
the monastery	*a kolostor*	o koloshtorr
the offertory	*a gyüjtés*	o dyĕŭytehsh
papal	*pápai*	pahpoi
the Pope	*a pápa*	o pahpo
a prayer	*imádság*	imahdshahg
prayer-book [man	*imádságos-könyv*	imahdshahgosh-kĕrnyv
the priest, clergy-	*a pap, lelkész*	o pop, lalkehss
a Protestant	*protestáns*	proteshtahnsh
the pulpit	*a szószék*	o sohsehk
Roman Catholic	*római-katholikus*	rohmoi-kotolikŏŏsh

English.	Hungarian.	Pronunciation.
the sacrament	*a szentség*	o santshehg
sacred	*szent*	sant
service, divine	*istentisztelet*	ishtantistalat
—, morning	*reggeli istentisztelet*	rag-gali ishtantistalat
—. evening	*esti* ,,	ashti ishtantistalat
vespers	*vecsernye*	vatcherrn-ya

Professions and Trades. (*Hivatal és foglalkozás.*)

(For Shopping see p. 97.)

An artist	*művész*	mïuvehss
a baker	*pék*	pehk
a banker	*bankár*	bonkahrr
a barber	*borbély*	borrbeh-y'
a bookbinder	*könyvkötő*	kĕrnyvkĕrter
a bookseller	*könyvárus*	kĕrnyv-ahrŏŏsh
a butcher	*mészáros*	mehsahrosh
a carpenter	*ács*	ahch
a cashier	*pénztáros*	pehnztahrosh
a clergyman	*lelkész*	lalkehss
a clerk	*irnok*	irrnok
a consul	*konzul*	konzŏŏl
a cook	*szakács*	sokahch
a cycle-maker	*kerékpár-készítő*	kerrehkpahrr-kehseeter
an engineer	*gépész*	geh-pehss
a fishmonger	*halárus*	holahrŏŏsh
a florist	*virágárus*	virahgahrŏŏsh
a glazier	*üveges*	e͡ŭvagesh
a goldsmith	*aranyműves*	orrony-mïuvash
a governess	*nevelőnő*	navalerner
the hatter	*a kalapos*	o koloposh
a jeweller	*ékszerész*	ehkserrehss
a lady's maid	*komorna*	komorrno
the laundress	*a mosónő*	o moshohner
a mason	*kőműves*	kermïuvash
a merchant	*kereskedő*	ka-rash-keder
a messenger	*követ*	kĕrvat
a miller	*molnár*	molnahrr
a nurse-maid	*dajka-leány*	doyko-leahny
an optician	*szemüveges*	same͡ŭvagesh
a photographer	*fényképész*	fehnykehpehss
a physician	*orvos*	orrvosh

English.	Hungarian.	Pronunciation.
a policeman	*rendőr*	randerr
the postmaster	*a postamester*	poshtomashterr
a printer	*nyomdász*	nyomdahss
a professor	*tanár*	tonahrr
a saddler	*nyereggyártó*	nya-reg-dyahrtoh
a schoolmaster	*tanító*	tonitoh
a servant	*cseléd*	chalehd
a shoemaker	*varga*	vorrgo
a shopkeeper	*boltos*	bol-tosh
a smith	*kovács*	kovahch
a soldier	*katona*	kotono
a solicitor	*ügyvéd*	e͡üdyvehd
a student	*tanuló*	tonŏŏloh
a tailor	*szabó*	soboh
a workman	*munkás*	mŏŏnkahsh

Legal Terms. (*Jogi fogalmak.*)

(For Conversations see p. 108)

The accused	*a vádlott*	o vahdlott
acquittal	*felmentés*	falmantehsh
to advance (money)	*előlegezni*	alerlagezni
an agreement	*kiegyezés*	kiedyazehsh
an alibi	*máshollét*	mahsh-holleht
to allege	*állítni*	ahlleetni
an apology	*bocsánatkérés*	botchahnotkehrehsh
to appeal	*fellebbezni*	fallabbezni
arrangement, agreement	*közvetités*	kĕrzvatitehsh
arrears	*hátralék*	hahtrolehk
to arrest	*letartóztatni*	letorrtohztotni
to attest	*bizonyítni*	bizonyeetni
attorney	*ügyvéd*	e͡üdyvehd
to authorise	*meghatalmazni*	meghotolmozni
an award	*itélet*	itehlat
to award	*odaitélni*	odo-itehlni
bail	*jótállás*	yohtahllahsh
bailiff	*elöljáró*	elerl-yahroh
bond (for loan)	*kötlevél, váltó*	kĕrtlavehl, vahltoh
case (suit)	*ügy* [*dolni*	e͡üdy [dolni
to charge	(*meg*) *terhelni, vá-*	(meg) terr-halni, vah-
client	*ügyfél*	e͡üdyfehl

English.	Hungarian.	Pronunciation.
the complainant	*a panaszos*	o ponososh
contract	*szerződés*	serrzerdehsh
a conviction	*rábizonyítás*	rahbizon-yeetahsh
costs	*ár, kiadás*	ahrr, kiodahsh
court of justice	*(kivételes) bíróság*	(kivehtalesh) beeroh-shahg
a criminal	*bűnös*	biunĕrsh
damages	*kárpótlás*	kahrrpohtlahsh
decision (of case)	*döntés*	dĕrntehsh
deed	*egyesség, cselekmény*	ed-yesh-shehg, chalak-mehny
to defend	*védni, (meg) védelmezni*	vehdni (meg), vehdal-mazni
defendant (in a suit)	*(jogi) vádlott*	(yog-i) vahdlott
document	*okirat*	okirot
evidence	*bizonyíték*	bizon-yeetehk
execution (of deed)	*elkészités*	alkehsitehsh
— (of judgment)	*bírói zár alá vevés és eladás*	beeroh-i zahrr olah vev-ehsh ehsh alodahsh
executor	*végrehajtó*	vehgra-hoytoh
fee (of office)	*díj*	dee-y'
fine (penalty)	*bírság*	beer-shahg
information, to give	*felvilágosítást adni*	falvilahgosheetahst odni
informer	*értesítő*	ehrtasheeter
injunction	*(bírói) végzés*	beeroh-i vehgzehsh
inventory	*leltár*	laltahrr
jail	*fogház*	fog-hahz
the judge	*a bíró*	o beeroh
jurisdiction	*törvénykezés*	tĕrrvehny-kazehsh
jurisprudence	*jogtudomány*	yogtŏŏdomahny
law-suit	*ügy*	e͡udy
oath, to take an	*esküdni (ik)*	ashke͡udni (ik)
parchment	*pergament*	perrgoment
pardon	*bocsánat, kegyelem*	botchahnot, kad-yal-em
penal	*büntető*	be͡untater
perjury	*hamis esküvés*	homish ashke͡uvehsh
petitioner	*kérelmező*	kehralmazer
police office	*rendőri hivatal*	randerri hivotol
— officer	*endőrtiszt*	randerrtist
— station	*rendőr állomás*	randerr ahllomahsh
proof	*próba, megvizsgálás*	prohbo, meg-vizh-gah-lahsh
to prosecute	*vádolni*	vahdolni
prosecution (of suit)	*vád*	vahd
prosecutor	*vádló*	vahdloh

English.	Hungarian.	Pronunciation.
punishment	*megbüntetés*	megbe͡untatehsh
to quash	*szétzúzni*	sehtzoozni
robbery	*rablás*	roblahsh
a seal	*pecsét*	patcheht
a sentence	*elitélés, bünösnek kimondás*	alitehlehsh, be͡unĕrsh-nak kimondahsh
statement (written)	*állítás*	ahlleetahsh
to sue	*üldözni, pörbe fogni*	e͡uldĕrzni, pĕrr-ba fogni
suit	*ügy*	e͡udy
summons (of court)	*megidézés*	meg-idehzehsh
testator	*végrendelkező*	vehgrandelkazer
theft	*lopás*	lopahsh
thief	*tolvaj*	tolvoy
trial	*próba, kisérlet*	prohbo, kishehrrlat
verdict	*ítélet*	eetehlat
witness	*tanú*	tonoo
writ	*idézés*	idehzehsh

Commercial and Trading.

(*Kereskedelmi és üzleti fogalmak.*)

(For Conversations see p 109.)

English.	Hungarian.	Pronunciation.
Account, to settle an	*kiegyenlíteni számlát*	ki-ed-yan-leetani sahmlaht
—, to close	*lezárni számlat*	lezahrni sahmlaht
—, current	*folyó számla*	foyoh sahmlo
—, joint	*részes számla*	rehsash sahmlo
— of sale	*eladási számla*	alodahshi sahmlo
acknowledgment	*elismervény*	alishmerrvehny
advance (money)	*kölcsön*	kĕrlchĕrn
advice, letter of	*értesítvény*	ehrtasheetvehny
agency	*ügynökség*	e͡udynĕrkshehg
the agent	*az ügynök*	oz e͡udynĕrk
the arrangement	*a megállapodás*	o megahllopodahsh
arrear, in	*hátrálék (ban)*	haltrahlehk (bon)
the assets	*az érték*	oz ehrrtehk
to authorise	*meghatalmazni*	meg-hotolmozni
the average	*az átlag*	oz ahtlog
the balance	*a mérleg*	o mehrrlag
balance of account	*a mérleg számla*	mehrrlag sahmlo
— -sheet	*mérlegív*	mehrrlag-eev
the bank	*a bank*	o bonk
the bearer	*az előmutató*	oz alermŏŏtotoh

English.	Hungarian.	Pronunciation.
bill, an accommo-	*kötött váltó*	kĕrtĕrtt vahltoh
bill at sight [dation	*váltó látásra*	vahltoh lahtahshro
— at 3 months'	*három hónapra*	hahrom hohnopro asha-
date	*esedékes váltó*	dehkash vahltoh
— of lading	*fuvar-elismervény*	föövorr-alishmerrvehny
the drawer	*az intéző*	oz intehzer
the drawee	*az intézvényezett*	oz intehzvehn-yezett
the bond	*a kötvény*	o kĕrtvehny
bond, in	*vámőrizet alatt*	vahmerrizat olott
bonded goods	*— alatti áruk*	vahmerrizat olotti ah-
the brokerage	*az alkuszdíj*	oz olkööss-dee-y' [röök
the business, retail	*az üzlet, kicsinybeni*	oz ëüzlat, kitchiny-bani
—, wholesale	*—, nagybani*	oz ëüzlat, nodyboni
the buyer	*a vevő*	o vever
the catalogue	*az árjegyzék*	oz ahrr-yady-zehk
to charter a ship	*hajót bérelni*	hoyoht behrelni [ba
to send in a claim	*követelést mutatni be*	kĕrvatalehsht möötotni
the clearing-house	*a leszámitoló bank*	o lessahmitoloh bonk
the clerk	*az írnok*	oz eernok
company	*társaság*	tahrshoshahg
—, limited	*részvény-társaság*	rehss-vehny-tahrsho-
the contract	*a szerződés*	o serrzerdehsh [shahg
cost, insurance and	*költség, biztosítás és*	kĕrltshehg, biztoshee-
freight	*viteldíj*	tahsh ehsh vitaldee-y'
a credit balance	*hitel mérleg*	hital mehrrlag
a creditor	*hitelező*	hitalezer
the custom-house	*a vámház*	o vahmhahz
the customs duties	*vámok*	vahmok
damages, compen-	*kártalanítás, kár-*	kahrtoloneetahsh,
sation	*pótlás*	kahrpohtlahsh
debit and credit	*tartozás és követelés*	torrtozahsh ehsh kĕr-
the debtor	*az adós*	oz odohsh [vatalehsh
to deliver	*szállítani*	sahlleetoni
delivered free	*bérmentve szállítani*	behrmantva sahlleetoni
the demurrage	*fekbér*	fakbehrr
the discount	*a leszámítolás*	lessahmeetolahsh
to discount [dues	*leszámítolni*	lessahmeetolni [kak
dock and harbour	*dokk és rév illetékek*	dokk ehsh rehv illateh-
double entry	*kettős könyvvitel*	kattersh kĕrnyv-vital
duty free	*vámmentes*	vahmmantash
—, liable to	*vám köteles*	vahm kĕrtalash

English.	Hungarian.	Pronunciation.
enclosed	*mellékelt*	mallehkalt
an enclosure	*melléklet*	mallehklat
to endorse	*hátiratolni*	hahtirotolni
the exchange	*a börze*	o bérr-za
the firm	*a cég*	o tsehg
forwarding agent	*szállítási ügynök*	sahlleetahshi e͡udyněrk
free on board	*szabadon a hajóra* [*rakva*	sobodon o hoyohro rok- [vo
gross weight	*elegysúly*	aladyshooy
import and export	*behozatal és kivitel*	ba-hozotol ehsh kivatal
the information	*az értesítés*	oz ehrtasheetehsh
insurance, marine	*hajókár biztosítás*	hoyohkahrr biztoshee-tahsh [vehny
— policy	*biztosítási kötvény*	biztosheetahshi kěrt-
— premium	— *díj*	biztosheetahshi dee-y'
to insure against	*biztosítani*	biztosheetoni
interest, rate of	*kamatláb*	komotlahb
the liabilities	*tartozások*	tortozahshok
to load	*megrakni*	megrokni
the market	*a vásár*	o vahshahrr
market, the cattle	*marha vásár*	morr-ho vahshahrr
—, the foreign	*külföldi piac*	ke͡ulfěrldi piots
—, the home	*belföldi piac*	balfěrldi piots
—, the London	*londoni piac*	londoni piots
the market day	*a vásár napja*	o vahshahrr nop-yo
— dues	— *illeték*	o vahshahrr illatehk
negotiable, saleable	*eladható*	alod-hotoh
net weight	*tiszta súly*	tisto shooy
to offer for sale	*eladásra kinálni*	alodahshro kinahlni
to order	*rendelni*	rendelni
the packing	*a becsomagolás*	o batchomogolahsh
the partnership	*az üzlettársi viszony*	oz e͡uzlattahrshi vissony
port of delivery	*kirakodó hely*	kirrokodoh hey
price, cost	*költség ár*	kěrltshehg ahrr
—, market	*piaci érték*	piotsi ehrrtehk
—, wholesale	*nagybani ár*	nodyboni ahrr
— -list [price)	*árjegyzék*	ahrr-yady-zehk
the quotation (of	*az árjelzés*	oz ahrr-yalzehsh
the receipt	*az átvétel* [*fogat*	oz ahtvehtal [fogot
registered tonnage	*bejegyzett tonnatér-*	ba-yadyzett tonnotehrr-
the registration	*a bejegyzés*	o ba-yadyzehsh
the rent	*a bérleti díj*	o behrlati dee-y'

English.	Hungarian.	Pronunciation.
the representative	*a megbizott* [*ok*	o meg-bizott
the settling days	*az elszámolási nap-*	oz alsahmolahshi nopok
shareholder	*részvényes*	rehssvehn-yesh
shares	*részvények* [*nyek*	rehssvehn-yek [vehn-yek
—, debenture	*kötelezvény rész vé-*	kĕrtalazvehny rehss-
—, preference	*elsőbbségi részvények*	alsherbbshehgi "
to ship	*szállítani* (*hajón*)	sahlleetoni (hoyohn)
shipping charges	*hajózási árak*	hoyohzahshi ahrok
solvent	*fizetőképes*	fizaterkehpash
the stock (security)	*a tőke* (*biztosíték*)	o ter-ka (biztosheetehk)
telegraphic address	*távirati cím*	tahviroti tsim
the towing charges	*a vontatási árak*	o vontotahshi ahrok
the trade	*a kereskedelem*	o ka-rash-kedalem
the underwriter	*a hajóbiztos*	o hoyohbiztosh
the unloading	*a hajórév*	o hoyoh-rehv
the wharfage	*partvám*	porrtvahm

Post Office, Telegraph and Telephone.

(*Póstahivatal, Távirat és Telefon.*)

(For Conversations see p. 103.)

Book post	*könyvpósta*	kĕrnyv-pohshto
contents	*tartalom*	torrtolom
counterfoil	*az ellenjegy*	oz allan-yady [dee-y'
excess postage	*túlságos póstadíj*	toolshahgosh pohsh-to-
insured value	*biztosított érték*	biztosheetott ehrrtehk
letter post	*levélpósta*	lavehl-pohshto
money order	*pósta-utalvány*	pohshto-ŏŏtolvahny
newspaper wrapper	*hírlap boríték*	hirrlop borreetehk
parcel post	*csomagpósta*	chomog-pohshto
post card	*levelező-lap*	lavalazer-lop
postage paid	*póstadíj fizetve*	pohshtodee-y' fizatva
the postman	*levélhordó*	lavehl-horrdoh
the postmaster	*a póstamester*	o pohshtomashterr
to re-address	*ujra címezni*	ŏŏyro tseemazni
to register	*ajánlva küldeni*	oyahnlvo keuldani
reply-paid	*válasz fizetve*	vahloss fizatva
stamp	*levélbélyeg*	lavehl-beh-yeg
telegraph form	*sürgönylap*	sheurr-ghĕrny-lop
— messenger	*sürgöny kihordó*	sheurr-ghĕrny ki-horr-
— office	*távíró hivatal*	tahveeroh hivotol [doh
weight, over	*túlsúly*	toolshooy

Correspondence. (*Levelezés.*)

(For Conversations see p. 107.)

English.	Hungarian.	Pronunciation.
The address	*a cím*	o tseem
blotting-paper	*itatós papiros*	itotohsh popirosh
the book	*a könyv*	o kěrnyv
the date	*a kelet*	o kalat
an enclosure	*melléklet*	mallehklat
an envelope	*boríték*	borreetehk
a fountain-pen	*töltő toll*	těrlter tol
the ink	*a tinta*	o tinto
an inkstand	*tintás üveg*	tintahsh e͡uvag
the letter	*a levél*	o lavehl
the letter-box	*a levélszekrény*	o lavehl-sekrehny
a note	*rövid levél*	rěrvid lavehl
the note-paper	*a levél papiros*	o lavehl popirosh
a steel pen	*acéltoll*	otsehltol
the pencil	*az irón*	oz irohn
a penholder	*tollszár*	tol-sahrr
a penknife	*tollkés*	tol-kehsh
a quire	*konc*	konts
a ream	*rizsma*	rizhmo
the scissors	*az olló*	o olloh
the seal	*a pecsétnyomó*	o patcheht-nyomoh
the sealing-wax	*a pecsétviasz*	o patcheht-vioss
a sheet (of paper)	*ív papiros*	eev popirosh
the signature	*az aláírás*	oz olah-eerahsh
the writing	*az írás*	oz eerahsh
— materials	*az írószerek*	oz irohserrek

Cardinal Numbers. (*Sarkszámok.*)

	Hungarian.	Pronunciation.		Hungarian.	Pronunciation.
1	*egy*	edy	10	*tíz*	teez
2	*kettő*, *két*	katter, keht	11	*tizenegy*	tiz-en-edy
3	*három*	hahrom	12	*tizenkettő**	tizenkatter
4	*négy*	nehdy	13	*tizenhárom*	tizenhahrom
5	*öt*	ěrt	14	*tizennégy*	tizennehdy
6	*hat*	hot	15	*tizenöt*	tizeněrt
7	*hét*	heht	16	*tizenhat*	tizenhot
8	*nyolc*	nyolts	17	*tizenhét*	tizenheht
9	*kilenc*	kilants	18	*tizennyolc*	tizen-nyolts

* Or *két*.

	Hungarian.	Pronunciation.
19	*tizenkilenc*	tizenkilants
20	*húsz*	hooss
21	*huszon-egy*	hŏŏs-on-edy
22	— *-kettő**	hŏŏsonkatter
23	— *-három*	hŏŏsonhahrom
24	— *-négy*	hŏŏson-nehdy
25	— *-öt*	hŏŏsonĕrt
26	— *-hat*	hŏŏsonhot
27	— *-hét*	hŏŏsonheht
28	— *-nyolc*	hŏŏson-nyolts
29	— *-kilenc*	hŏŏson-kilants
30	*harminc*	horrmints
40	*negyven*	nadyvan
50	*ötven*	ĕrtvan
60	*hatvan*	hotvon
70	*hetven*	hatvan
80	*nyolcvan*	nyoltsvon

	Hungarian.	Pronunciation.
90	*kilencven*	kilantsvan
100	*száz*	sahz
101	*száz egy*	sahz edy
110	*száz tíz*	sahz teez
120	*száz húsz*	sahz hooss
130	*száz harminc*	sahz horr-mints
200	*két száz*	keht sahz
300	*három száz*	hahrom sahz
400	*négy száz*	nehdy sahz
500	*öt száz*	ĕrt sahz
600	*hat száz*	hot sahz
700	*hét száz*	heht sahz
800	*nyolc száz*	nyolts sahz
900	*kilenc száz*	kilants sahz
1000	*ezer*	azerr
1910	*ezer kilenc száz tíz*	azerr kilants sahz teez

Ordinal Numbers. (*Sorszámnevek.*)

English.	Hungarian.	Pronunciation.
First	*első*	alsher
second	*második*	mahshodik
third	*harmadik*	horrmodik
fourth	*negyedik*	nad-yadik
fifth	*ötödik*	ĕrtĕrdik
sixth	*hatodik*	hotodik
seventh	*hetedik*	hatadik
eighth	*nyolcadik*	nyoltsodik
ninth	*kilencedik*	kilantsadik
tenth	*tizedik*	tizadik
eleventh	*tizenegyedik*	tizenedyadik
twelfth	*tizenkettedik*	tizenkattadik
thirteenth	*tizenharmadik*	tizenhorrmodik
fourteenth	*tizennegyedik*	tizennadyadik
fifteenth	*tizenötödik*	tizenĕrtĕrdik
sixteenth	*tizenhatodik*	tizenhotodik
seventeenth	*tizenhetedik*	tizenhatadik
eighteenth	*tizennyolcadik*	tizennyoltsodik
nineteenth	*tizenkilencedik*	tizenkilantsadik
twentieth	*huszadik*	hŏŏsodik

* Or *két.*

English.	Hungarian.	Pronunciation.
twenty-first	*huszonegyedik*	hŏŏsoned-yadik
thirtieth	*harmincadik*	horrmintsodik
fortieth	*negyvenedik*	ned*y*vanadik
fiftieth	*ötvenedik*	ĕ*r*tvanadik
sixtieth	*hatvanadik*	hotvonodik
seventieth	*hetvenedik*	hatvanadik
eightieth	*nyolcvanadik*	n*y*oltsvonodik
ninetieth	*kilencvenedik*	kilantsvanadik
hundredth	*századik*	sahzodik
thousandth	*ezredik*	azradik
last	*utolsó*	ŏŏtolshoh

Collective Numbers, &c. (*Gyüjtőszámok.*)

A couple, pair	*egy pár*	ed*y* pahrr
double	*kétszeres*	kehtserresh
a dozen	*egy tucat*	ed*y* tŏŏtsot
the first time	*először*	ale*r*sĕ*r*r
a fifth	*egy ötöd*	ed*y* ĕ*r*tĕ*r*d
firstly	*először*	ale*r*sĕ*r*r
the half	*a fél*	o fehl
once	*egyszer*	ed*y*serr
one sort	*egyféle*	ed*y*fehla
a part	*egy rész*	ed*y* rehss
a score	*húsz (egyben)*	hooss (ed*y*ban)
secondly	*másodszor*	mahshodsorr
the second time	*másodízben*	mahshodeezban
simple	*egyszerű*	ed*y*serrïu
singly	*egyenként*	ed-yan-kehnt
a third	*egy harmad*	ed*y* horrmod
thirdly	*harmadszor*	horrmodsorr
threefold	*háromszoros*	hahromsorrosh
three-sevenths	*három heted*	hahrom hatad
twice	*kétszer*	kehtserr
two-sixths	*két hatod*	keht hotod

Adjectives. (*Melléknevek.*)

(For Grammar of Adjectives see p. 70.)

Arrogant	*öntelt*	ĕ*r*ntalt
bad	*rossz*	ross
bitter	*keserű*	kasherrïu
blind	*vak*	vok
blunt (tool, etc.)	*tompa*	tompo

English.	Hungarian.	Pronunciation.
bold	*merész, vakmerő*	ma-rehss, vokma-rer
brave	*bátor*	bahtorr
brisk	*élénk*	ehlehnk
broad	*széles*	sehlash
certain	*bizonyos*	bizonyosh
cheap	*olcsó*	olchoh
clean	*tiszta*	tisto
clear	*világos*	vilahgosh
clever	*okos*	okosh
cold	*hideg*	hidag
content	*elégedett*	alehg-edett
cowardly	*gyáva*	dyahvo
dark	*sötét*	shĕrteht
deaf	*süket*	sheūkat
dear (beloved)	*kedves*	kadvash
— (costly)	*drága*	drahgo
deep	*mély*	meh-y'
dirty	*piszkos*	piskosh
disagreeable	*kellemetlen*	kallamatlan
dishonest	*tisztességtelen*	tistash-shehg-talan
drunken	*részeg*	rehseg
dry	*száraz*	sahroz
dumb	*néma*	nehmo
dusty	*poros*	porrosh
early (fruit)	*korai (gyümölcs)*	korro-i (dyeūmĕrlch)
easy	*könnyü, kényelmes*	kĕrnnyeū,kehn-yalmash
equal	*egyenlő*	ed-yan-ler
fair	*szép, szőke, világos*	sehp, serka, vilahgosh
faithless	*hűtlen*	hīutlan
false	*hamis*	homish
fat	*kövér*	kĕrvehrr
fierce	*szilaj, vad*	siloy, vod
fit	*alkalmas*	olkolmosh
flat	*lapos*	loposh
foolish	*bolondos*	bolondosh
free	*szabad*	sob-od
frequent	*gyakori*	dyokorri
fresh	*friss, üde*	frish, eūda
full	*tele*	ta-la
gay	*víg*	veeg
gentle	*gyöngéd, nyájas*	dyĕrnghehd, nyah-yosh

English.	Hungarian.	Pronunciation.
good	*jó*	yoh
great	*nagy*	nody
hairy	*hajas, szőrös*	hoyosh, serrĕrsh
handsome	*szép, deli*	sehp, dal-i
happy	*boldog, szerencsés*	bol-dog, serren-chehsh
hard	*kemény*	kam-ehny
heavy	*nehéz, súlyos*	na-hehz, shoo-yosh
high	*magas*	mogosh
hollow	*üres*	e͡urash
honest	*becsületes, tisztessé-* [*ges*	batche͡ulatesh, tistash- [shehg-esh
hot	*forró*	forroh
hungry	*éhes*	eh-hash
ill	*rossz*	ross
impolite	*udvariatlan*	ŏŏdvorriotlon
innocent	*ártatlan*	ahrrtotlon
just	*igazságos*	igoz-shahgosh
lame	*sánta*	shahnto
large	*nagy*	nody
late	*késő*	keh-sher
lean	*sovány*	shovahny
light	*világos*	vilahgosh
long	*hosszú*	hossoo
loose	*laza*	lozzo
muddy	*sáros*	shahrosh
narrow	*szoros, keskeny*	sorrosh, keshkeny
new	*új*	ooy
oblong	*hosszukás*	hossŏŏkahsh
old	*öreg*	ĕrrag
open	*nyílt*	nyeelt
polite	*udvarias*	ŏŏdvorriosh
poor	*szegény*	sag-ehny
pretty	*csinos*	chinosh
private	*magán, egyéni*	mogahn, edyehni
proud	*büszke*	be͡uss-ka
public	*nyilvános*	nyilvahnosh
pure	*tiszta*	tisto
quiet	*nyugalmas*	nyŏŏgolmosh
rich	*gazdag*	gozdog
ripe	*érett*	ehrett
rough	*durva, göröngyös*	dŏŏrvo, ghĕrrĕrndyĕrsh
round	*kerek, gömbölyű*	ka-rak, ghĕrmbĕrl-yïu

English.	Hungarian.	Pronunciation.
sacred	*szent*	sant
sad	*szomorú*	somorroo
sharp	*éles*	ehlash
short	*rövid*	rěrvid
slow	*lassú*	losh-shoo
small	*kicsi*	kitchi
smooth	*síma*	sheemo
soft	*lágy*	lahdy
sound	*egészséges*	ag-ehss-shehg-esh
sour	*savanyú*	shovon-yoo
square	*négyszögletű*	nehdyserglatïu
strange	*idegen*	id-ag-en
strong	*erős*	a-rersh
stupid	*ostoba*	oshtobo
sweet	*édes*	ehdesh
swift	*gyors*	dyorsh
tall	*magas*	mogosh
tender	*puha, gyöngéd*	pŏŏ-ho, dyěrn-ghehd
thick	*vastag, sűrű*	voshtog, shïurïu
thin	*vékony*	vehkony
thirsty	*szomjas*	som-yosh
timely	*időszerű*	iderserrïu
troublesome	*alkalmatlan, zavaró*	olkolmotlon, zovorroh
true	*igaz*	i-goz
ugly	*csunya*	chŏŏn-yo
uncertain	*bizonytalan*	bizony-tolon
unequal	*egyenlőtlen*	ed-yan-lertlan
unfit	*alkalmatlan*	olkolmotlon
unsettled	*rendezetlen*	rendezatlan
useful	*hasznos*	hossnosh
vain	*hiú, üres*	hioo, e͡urash
warm	*meleg*	malag
weak	*gyönge*	dyěrn-ga
well	*jól*	yohl
wet	*nedves*	nadvash
whole	*egész*	ag-ehss
wide	*széles*	sehlash
wild	*vad*	vod
wise	*bölcs, okos, tudós*	běrlch, okosh, tŏŏdohsh
young	*fiatal*	fiotol

Verbs.* (*Igék.*)

(For Grammar of Verbs see pp. 73—81.)

English.	Hungarian.	Pronunciation.
To accept	*elfogadni*	alfogodni
,, admire	*bámulni*	bahmŏŏlni
,, affirm	*állítani*	ahlleetoni
,, answer	*válaszolni*	vahlosolni
,, approve	*helyeselni*	heyeshelni
,, arrive	*megérkezni* (*ik*)	meg-ehrrkezni (ik)
,, ascend	*felmenni*	falmanni
,, ask	*kérdezni*	kehrdezni
,, assure	*biztosítani*	biztosheetoni
,, awake	(*fel*) *ébredni*	fal (ehbradni)
,, be	*van* (*lenni*)	von (lenni)
,, be hungry	*éhezni* (*ik*)	eh-hazni (ik)
,, beat	*ütni*	e͡utni
,, begin	*kezdeni*	kazdani
,, believe	*hinni*	hinni
,, blame	*hibáztatni, feddni*	hibahztotni, faddni
,, boil	*forralni, főzni*	forrolni, ferzni
,, borrow	*kölcsönvenni*	kĕrlchĕrnvenni
,, breakfast	*reggelizni* (*ik*)	reg-galizni (ik)
,, bring	*hozni*	hozni
,, build	*építeni*	ehpeetani
,, buy	*venni*	venni
,, calculate	*kiszámitani*	kissahmitoni
,, carry	*hordani*	horrdoni
,, chat	*beszélgetni, fecsegni*	bassehlgatni, fatchagni
,, compare	*összehasonlitani*	ĕrssa-hoshonlitoni
,, consent	*beleegyezni* (*ik*)	bala-ed-yazni (ik)
,, continue	*folytatni*	foytotni
,, cook	*főzni*	ferzni
,, cough	*köhögni*	kĕrhĕrgni
,, cover	*fedni, betakarni*	fadni, batokorrni
,, dance	*táncolni*	tahntsolni
,, deny	*tagadni*	togodni
,, depart	*elutazni* (*ik*)	alŏŏtozni (ik)
,, descend	*leszállni*	lessahlni
,, desire	*kivánni*	kivahnni

* The infinitive of all Hungarian verbs ends with *ni*; the dictionaries put the verbs in the third person singular, to which one adds *ni* to obtain the infinitive.

English.	Hungarian.	Pronunciation.
to despise	*megvetni*	megvatni
,, dine	*ebédelni*	abehdelni
,, dispute	*vitatkozni*	vitotkozni
,, do	*tenni, csinálni*	tenni, chinahlni
,, doubt	*kétkedni (ik)*	kehtkedni (ik)
,, draw (pull)	*húzni*	hoozni
— (attract)	*vonzani*	vonzoni
,, dream	*álmodni (ik)*	ahlmodni (ik)
,, dress, *intr.*	*öltözni (ik)*	ĕrltĕrzni (ik)
—, *trans.*	*öltöztetni*	ĕrltĕrztatni
,, drink	*inni (ik)*	inni (ik)
,, eat	*enni (ik)*	enni (ik)
,, embrace	*ölelni*	ĕrlalni
,, esteem	*tisztelni, becsülni*	tistelni, batche͡ulni
,, estimate	*megbecsülni*	megbatche͡ulni
,, exchange	*kicserélni*	kitcherrehlni
,, exclaim	*felkiáltani*	falkiahltoni
,, excuse	*kimenteni*	kimantani
,, explain	*magyarázni, fejte-*	mod-yorrahzni, feyte-
,, fall	*elesni (ik)* [*getni*	alashni (ik) [gatni
,, feel	*érezni*	ehrezni
,, find	*találni*	tolahlni
,, finish	*bevégezni*	bavehgazni
,, flatter	*hízelegni*	heezalegni
,, follow	*követni*	kĕrvatni
,, forget	*elfelejteni*	alfaleytani
,, get up	*felkelni*	falkalni
,, give	*adni*	odni
,, go	*menni, járni*	menni, yahrrni
,, go in	*bemenni*	bamenni
,, go out	*kimenni*	kimenni
,, grow, *intr.*	*nőlni*	nerlni
—, *trans.*	*termelni*	terrmalni
,, hate	*gyűlölni*	dyïulĕrlni
,, have	*birni, (van neki)*	birrni, (von naki)
,, hear	*hallani*	holloni
,, hide	*elrejteni*	alreytani
,, honour	*tisztelni*	tistalni
,, hope	*remélni*	ramehlni
,, imagine	*képzelni*	kehpzalni
,, imitate	*utánozni*	ŏŏtahnozni

English.	Hungarian.	Pronunciation.
to insult	*megsérteni*	megshehrrtani
,, joke	*tréfálni*	trehfahlni
,, jump	*ugrani (ik)*	ŏŏgroni (ik)
,, know	*tudni*	tŏŏdni
,, laugh	*nevetni*	navatni
,, lay a table-cloth	*teríteni (asztalt)*	terreetani (ostolt)
,, learn	*tanulni*	tonŏŏlni
,, lend	*kölcsönözni*	kĕrlchĕrnĕrzni
,, lie down	*lefeküdni (ik)*	lefakŏŏdni (ik)
,, live	*élni*	ehlni
,, look for	*keresni*	ka-rashni
,, lose	*elveszíteni*	alvasseetani
,, love	*szeretni*	serratni
,, maintain	*fenntartani*	fanntorrtoni
,, make	*csinálni, tenni*	chinahlni, tenni
,, meet	*találkozni (ik)*	tolahlkozni (ik)
,, be mistaken	*tévedni*	tehvadni
,, be ignorant of	*nem tudni*	nam tŏŏdni
,, object	*ellenezni*	allanezni
,, offend	*megsérteni*	megshehrrtani
,, open	*kinyitni*	kin-yitni
,, pack up	*becsomagolni*	batchomogolni
,, paint	*festeni*	fashtani
,, pardon	*megbocsátani*	megbotchahtoni
,, pay	*fizetni*	fizatni
,, plant	*ültetni*	e͡ultatni
,, play	*játszani (ik)*	yahtsoni (ik)
,, pluck(goose,&c.)	*húzni, kopasztani*	hoozni, kopostoni
,, praise	*dicsérni* [*tatni*	ditchehrrni [totni
,, present	*ajándékozni, bemu-*	oyahndehkozni, bamŏŏ-
,, prove	*kipróbálni*	kiprohbahlni
,, punish	*megbüntetni*	megbe͡untatni
,, quarrel	*veszekedni (ik)*	vassakedni (ik)
,, be quiet	*lecsendesülni*	letchandashe͡ulni
,, read	*olvasni*	olvoshni
,, reap	*aratni*	orrotni
,, receive	*kapni, elfogadni*	kopni, alfogodni
,, reflect	*elmélkedni (ik)*	almehlkedni (ik)
— (light)	*visszaverni*	vissoverrni
,, refuse	*megtagadni*	megtogodni
regret	*sajnálni*	shoynahlni

English.	Hungarian.	Pronunciation.
to rejoice	*örvendezni (ik)*	ĕrrvandezni (ik)
,, remember	*emlékezni (ik)*	amlehkezni (ik)
,, repay	*visszafizetni*	vissofizatni
,, repeal	*eltörölni*	altĕrrĕrlni
,, repeat	*(meg) ismételni*	(meg) ishmehtelni
,, reply	*válaszolni*	vahlosolni
,, rest	*nyugodni (ik)*	nyŏŏ-godni (ik)
,, return (give back)	*visszaadni*	visso-odni
— (come back)	*visszatérni*	vissotehrrni
,, revenge	*megboszúlni*	megbosoolni
,, ring the bell	*csengetni*	chan-gatni
,, roast	*sütni*	sheutni
,, run	*szaladni, futni*	solodni, fŏŏtni
,, say	*mondani*	mondoni
,, scheme	*tervelni*	terrvalni
,, seal	*pecsételni*	patchehtelni
,, see	*látni*	lahtni
,, sell	*eladni*	alodni
,, serve	*szolgálni*	solgahlni
,, show	*mutatni*	mŏŏtotni
,, sigh	*sóhajtani*	shoh-hoytoni
,, sign	*jelezni*	yal-ezni
,, sip	*szörpölni*	sĕrrpĕrlni
,, sit down	*leülni*	le-eulni
,, sleep	*aludni (ik)*	olŏŏdni (ik)
,, sneeze	*tüsszenni*	teussanni
,, sow	*vetni, szórni*	vatni, sohrrni
,, speak	*beszélni*	bassehlni
,, spin	*fonni*	fonni
,, spoil	*elrontani, kifosztani*	alrontoni, kifostoni
,, steal	*lopni*	lopni
,, stitch	*öltögetni, varrni*	ĕrltĕrgatni, vorrni
,, study	*tanulni*	tonŏŏlni
,, swear	*esküdni (ik)*	ashkeudni (ik)
,, take	*elvenni, fogni*	alvenni, fogni
,, taste	*megízlelni*	meg-eezlalni
,, tell	*mondani*	mondoni
,, thank	*köszönni*	kĕrsĕrnni
,, think	*gondolni*	gondolni
,, be thirsty	*szomjazni (ik)*	som-yozni (ik)
,, throw	*dobni*	dobni

English.	Hungarian.	Pronunciation.
to touch	*érinteni*	ehrintani
,, translate	*lefordítani*	leforrdeetoni
,, travel	*utazni (ik)*	ŏŏtozni (ik)
,, uncover	*kitakarni*	kitokorrni
,, unpack	*kicsomagolni, kibontani*	kitchomogolni, kibontoni
,, wash	*mosni, mosdani (ik)*	moshni, moshdoni (ik)
,, weep	*sírni*	sheerrni
,, weigh	*emelni, mérlegelni*	amalni, mehrlagalni
,, wish	*kivánni*	kivahnni
,, will	*akarni*	okorrni
,, work	*dolgozni*	dolgozni
,, worship	*imádni*	imahdni
,, wrap	*beburkolni*	babŏŏrrkolni
,, write	*írni*	eerrni

Adverbs, Conjunctions and Prepositions.

(*Határozók, kötőszók és névutók.*)

(For Grammar see pp. 69, 81, 82.)

About	*körül*	kĕrre͡ul
above	*felett*	falatt
above all	*mindenekfelett*	mindenekfalatt
according to	*szerint*	serrint
after	*után*	ŏŏtahn
afterwards	*azután*	ozŏŏtahn
again	*újból*	ooybohl
against	*ellen*	allan
all at once	*egyszerre*	edyserra
almost	*majdnem*	moydnam
already	*már*	mahrr
also	*is*	ish
although	*bár*	bahrr
altogether	*egészben véve, együttesen*	ag-ehssban vehva, edye͡ut-ashan
always	*mindig*	mindig
among	*között*	kĕrzĕrt
and	*és*	ehsh
anywhere	*bárhol*	bahrr-hol
as	*mint*	mint
as much	*annyira, annyi mint*	onn-yirro, onn-yi mint
as soon as	*mihelyt*	mi-heyt
at	*nél*	nehl
at first	*eleinte*	al-a-in-ta

English.	Hungarian.	Pronunciation.
at last	*végre*	vehgra
at least	*legalább*	lagolahbb
at once	*egyszerre*	ed*y*serra
at present	*jelenleg*	yal-en-lag
badly	*rosszul*	rossŏŏl
because	*mert*	merrt
before	*előtt*	ale*r*tt
behind	*mögött*	mĕ*r*g-ĕ*r*tt
below, *adv.*	*alatt, lenn*	olott, lenn
besides, beyond	*mellett, kivül, túl*	mallatt, kivēūl, tool
better	*jobb*	yobb
between	*között*	kĕ*r*zĕ*r*tt
but	*de, azonban*	da, ozonbon
by, by the side of	*mellett*	mallatt
by turns	*felváltva*	falvahltvo
consequently	*következéskép*	kĕ*r*vatkezehshkehp
down	*le*	le
during	*alatt*	olott
early	*korán*	korrahn
either ... or	*vagy...vagy*	vod*y*...vod*y*
elsewhere	*máshol*	mahsh-hol
enough	*elég*	alehg
even if	*még akkor is, ha*	mehg okkorr ish, ho
everywhere	*mindenhol*	mindenhol
except, *conj.*	*hacsak...nem*	ho-chok...nam
—, *prep.*	*kivéve*	kivehva
except that	*kivéve, hogy*	kivehva, hod*y*
far	*messze*	massa
for, *prep.*	*ért*	ehrrt
—, *conj.*	*mert*	merrt
from	*ból, tól*	bohl, tohl
fully	*egészen, teljesen*	ag-ehssan, tal-yashan
hardly	*alig, nehezen*	olig, na-hazan
here	*itt*	itt
how	*hogy (an)*	hod*y* (on)
however, *conj.*	*azonban*	ozonbon
—, *adv.*	*bármilyen*	bahrr-mi-yan
if	*ha*	ho
immediately	*azonnal, közvetlenül*	ozonnol, kĕ*r*zvatlanēūl
in, within	*-ban, -ben, belül*	-bon, -ban, balēūl
in future	*ezentúl, a jövőben*	azentool, o yĕ*r*ve*r*ban

English.	Hungarian.	Pronunciation.
in spite of	*ellenére*	allanehra
in the midst of	*között*	kĕrzĕrtt
indeed	*valóban*	volohbon
inside	*benn, belül*	bann, baleu͡l
instead of	*helyett*	heyett
less	*kisebb, kevesebb*	kishabb, kavashabb
like	*hasonlóan, mint*	hoshonlohon, mint
little by little	*lassanként*	loshshonkẹhnt
many times	*sokszor, gyakran*	shoksorr, dyokron
more	*többet, inkább*	tĕrbbat, inkahbb
more and more	*egyre jobban, egyre* [*inkább*	edy-ra yobbon, edy-ra [inkahbb
much	*nagyon*	nod-yon
near	*közel*	kĕrzal
nearly	*csaknem, majdnem*	choknam, moydnam
neither ... nor	*sem...sem*	sham...sham
never	*soha*	sho-ho
next to	*mellett, majdnem*	mallatt, moydnam
not	*nem*	nam
not at all	*egyáltalában nem*	ed-yahltolahbon nam
not yet	*még nem*	mehg nam
now	*most, jelenleg*	mosht, yalenlag
nowhere	*sehol (sem)*	she-hol (sham)
of	*-tól, -ról*	-tohl, -rohl
of course	*természetesen, hogyne*	termmehssat-eshan, [hody-na
often	*gyakran*	dyokron
on account of	*-nál, -nél fogva*	-nahl, -nehl fogvo
on this side	*-n, -on, -en innen*	-n, -on, -en innen
only	*csak*	chok
opposite	*-val, -vel átellenben*	-vol, -val, ahtallanban
or	*vagy*	vody
otherwise, *adv.*	*másképen*	mahsh-kehpan
out of	*-ból, ki*	-bohl, ki
outside, *adv.*	*künn, kívül*	keu͡n, keeveu͡l
over	*fölött, át, túl*	fĕrlĕrtt, aht, tool
perhaps	*talán*	tolahn
presently, soon	*rögtön, nemsokára*	rĕrgtĕrn, namshokahrro
previously	*megelőzőleg*	megalerzerlag
quickly	*gyorsan, hirtelen*	dyorrshon, hirrtalan
rather	*inkább*	inkahbb
round about	*köröskörül*	kĕrrĕrshkĕrreu͡l
scarcely	*alig*	olig

English.	Hungarian.	Pronunciation.
seldom	*ritkán*	ritkahn
since, *prep.*	*óta*	ohto
—, *adv.*	*mivel, minthogy*	mival, mint-hody
—, *conj.*	*mivel*	mival
so	*olyan*	oyon
sometimes	*néha*	neh-ho
so much	*annyira* [*hamar*	onn-yirro [homorr
soon	*nemsokára, csak-*	namshokahro, chok-
suddenly	*hirtelen (ül)*	hirrtalan (eul)
that	*hogy, tegyük fel,*	hody, ted-yeuk fal,
that is	*vagyis* [*hogy...*	vod-yish [hody...
then, *adv.*	*akkor*	okkorr
—, *conj.*	*tehát*	te-haht
thence	*onnan*	onnon
there	*ott*	ott
through	*át, keresztül*	aht, ka-rass-teul
thus	*így, úgy*	eedy, oody
till, *conj.*	*(a)míg*	(o) meeg
—, *prep.*	*-ig*	-ig
to	*-nak, -ra, hoz*	-nok, -ro, -hoz
together	*együtt*	ed-yeutt
too much, *adv.*	*túlságos sok, túlsá-*	toolshahgosh shok, too-
towards	*felé* [*gosan*	fal-eh [shahgoshon
under	*alatt*	olott
unless	*kivéve, hacsak...nem*	kivehva, ho-chok...nam
until	*-ig (idő)*	-ig (ider)
up	*fel*	fal
upon	*-n, -on, -ön*	-n, -on, -ĕrn
	-ról, -ről, felől	-rohl, rerl, falerl
very, *adv.*	*nagyon*	nod-yon
well	*jól*	yohl
when	*mikor*	mikorr
where	*hol? hová?*	hol? hovah?
while, whilst	*míg, mialatt*	meeg, miolott
why?	*miért?*	mi-ehrrt?
willingly	*örömest, készségesen*	ĕrrĕrmasht, kehss-sheh-
with (near)	*-val*	-vol [gashan
within, *adv.*	*belül*	baleul
without, *prep.*	*kívül, nélkül*	keeveul, nehlkeul
without doubt	*kétségkívül*	kehtshehg-keeveul
yet	*mégis*	mehg-ish

ELEMENTARY GRAMMAR.

The Article. (*A Névelő.*)

There are two articles, the Definite and the Indefinite. The Definite Article is *a* for words beginning with a consonant, *az* for words beginning with a vowel.

The Indefinite Article is *egy*, which is also the numeral "one." It is not the exact equivalent of the English "a," "an," for it is usually omitted except when stress is laid on the singleness of the object, or in cases where its meaning is that of "a certain"; it must never be put before an adjective or noun used as a predicate.

e.g. *Van ebben a faluban vendéglő?* (not egy *vendéglő*).
Is there *an* inn in this village?

The Substantive. (*A Főnév.*)

Nouns ending with a vowel form their plural by adding *k*; the vowels *a* and *e* then become long, as *fa*, tree, *fák*, trees; *eke*, plough, *ekék*, ploughs. When a noun ends with a consonant, the plural is formed by adding *ak*, *ok*, *ek*, *ök*. If the consonant is preceded by *á* or *é*, then those vowels are shortened in the plural, excepting those ending in *ság*, *ség*, *gás*, *gés*, and a few monosyllabic nouns.

The vowel of the last syllable is dropped in the plural when the consonants *m-r*, *k-r*, *k-l*, *r-m*, *r-k* and *l-k* meet; as *lélek*, soul, *lelkek*, souls; *járom*, yoke, *jármok*, yokes.

The following nouns ending with a vowel take *j* or *v* in the plural, besides the usual plural ending:—*mű*, a work of art, *művek*, works of art; *tő*, stem, *tövek*, stems; *kő*, stones, *kövek*, stones; *cső*, a tube, *csövek*, tubes, *lé*, juice, *levek*, juices; *fű*, herb, *füvek*, herbs; *ló*, horse, *lovak*, horses.

If a noun is preceded by a numeral or any other word expressing quantity, then it is used only in the singular, as *két ember*, two men; *sok fa*, many trees.

The names of corn, metals, fruit, minerals, etc.—that is to say, all generic nouns—are collective nouns in Hungarian, and are used in the singular; as *körte*, a pear or pears; *szilva*, a plum or plums.

Declension.

Substantives are divided into six classes or declensions, the plural endings being taken as the basis for this division; then each class is divided into two, viz., with the short and the long vowels; as Class I., *ak*, *ák*; II., *ok*, *ók*; III., *uk*; IV. *ek*, *ék*; V., *ök*, *ők*; VI., *ük*.

* Respecting *gender*, see p. 84, third paragraph.

The suffixes for Classes I., II. and III. are: For Nominative, the name itself or with personal suffix; Attributive or Possessive, *nak*; Genitive, *é*; Dative, *nak*; Accusative, *t*.

The suffixes for Classes IV., V. and VI. for the same cases as above are: *nek*, *é*, *nek*, *t*.

Personal Suffixes.

The object governed by the attributive case is inflected, as *Péternek atyja*, Peter's father. There are in Hungarian four relations of the object to the possessor: 1. Object and possessor in *Singular*, as *könyv-em*, my book. 2. Object in *Singular* and possessor in *Plural*, as *könyv-ünk*, our book. 3. Object in *Plural* and possessor in *Singular*, as *könyv-eim*, my books. 4. Object and possessor in *Plural*, as *könyv-eink*, our books.

I. The Object in the SINGULAR:—*könyv-em*, my book; *könyv-ed*, thy book; *könyv-e*, his book; *könyv-ünk*, our book; *könyv-etek*, your book; *könyv-ük*, their book.

II. The Object in the PLURAL:—*könyv-eim*, my books; *könyv-eid*, thy books; *könyv-ei*, his books; *könyv-eink*, our books; *könyv-eitek*, your books; *könyv-eik*, their books.

THE PERSONAL SUFFIXES OF THE SIX DECLENSIONS.

The Object possessed in the *Singular*:—

I. Plural endings *ak*, *ák*. Sing. *am*, *ad*, *a*; *ám*, *ád*, *ája*. Plur. *unk*, *atok*, *uk*; *ánk*, *átok*, *ájok*.

II. Plural endings *ok*, *ók*. Sing. *om*, *od*, *a*; *óm*, *ód*, *ója*. Plur. *unk*, *otok*, *uk* (or *juk*); *ónk*, *ótok*, *ójuk*.

III. Plural ending *úk*. Sing. *úm*, *úd*, *úja*. Plur. *únk*, *útok*, *újok*.

IV. Plural endings *ek*, *ék*. Sing. *em*, *ed*, *e*; *ém*, *éd*, *éje*. Plur. *ünk*, *etek*, *ük*; *énk*, *étek*, *éjök*.

V. Plural endings *ök*, *ők*. Sing. *öm*, *öd*, *e*; *őm*, *őd*, *ője* or *eje*. Plur. *ünk*, *ötök*, *ük*; *őnk*, *őtök*, *őjök* or *ejük*.

VI. Plural ending *üm*. Sing. *üm*, *üd*, *üje*. Plur. *ünk*, *ütök*, *üjök*.

The Object possessed in the *Plural*:—

I. Plural endings *ak*, *ák*. Sing. *aim*, *aid*, *ai*; *áim*, *áid*, *ái*. Plur. *aink*, *aitok*, *aik*; *áink*, *áitok*, *áik*.

II. Plural endings *ok*, *ók*. Sing. *aim*, *aid*, *ai*; *óim*, *óid*, *ói*. Plur. *aink*, *aitok*, *aik*; *óink*, *óitok*, *óik*.

III. Plural ending *uk*. Sing. *úim*, *úid*, *úi*. Plur. *úink*, *úitok*, *úik*.

IV. Plural endings *ek*, *ék*. Sing. *eim*, *eid*, *ei*; *éim*, *éid*, *éi*. Plur. *eink*, *eitek*, *eik*; *éink*, *éitek*, *éik*.

V. Plural endings *ök*, *ők*. Sing. *eim*, *eid*, *ei*; *őim*, *őid*, *ői* or *ei*. Plur. *eink*, *eitek*, *eik*; *öink*, *őitek*, *őik* or *eik*.

VI. Plural ending *ük*. Sing. *üim*, *üid*, *üi*. Plur. *üink*, *üitek*, *üik*.

In order to be able to find to what declension a noun belongs, one has to form its plural ending; as *ökör*, an ox, plur. *ökrök*. Its ending *ök* indicates that its personal suffix is in Class V. The same rule one can apply for the monosyllabic nouns; as *atya*, father, *anya*, mother, *bátya*, elder brother, take in the third person sing. and plur. *ja* and *jok*, instead of *ája*, *ájok*, while *öcs*, younger brother, takes *cs* instead of *j*.

The genitive suffix *é* for all nouns expresses possession as well; as, *Ez a kalap Péteré*, this hat is Peter's.

Suffixes.

To indicate places and directions, instead of prepositions Hungarian has suffixes. They are classified as follows:—

1. Retaining or remaining: *ban ben*; as *ház-ban*, in the house.
2. Indicating: *on*, *en*, *ön*; as *ház-on*, on or upon the house—after a vowel only *n*: as *eke*, plough, *ekén*, on the plough.
3. Resting: *nál*, *nél*; as *ő atyám-nál van*, he is with my father.
4. Inward direction: *ba*, *be*; as *a ház-ba megyek*, I go into the house.
5. Upward direction: *ra*, *re*; as *tedd az asztal-ra*, put it on the table.
6. Approaching: *hoz*, *hez*, *höz*; as *ház-hoz*, to the house.
7. Outward direction: *ból*, *ből*; as *ki-vettem a kosár-ból*, I took it out of the basket.
8. Downward direction: *ról*, *ről*; as *a kémény leesett a ház-ról*, the chimney fell down from the house.
9. Moving or starting: *tól*, *től*; as *a ház-tól távozott*, he moved (or started) from the house.
10. Limiting: *ig*, as *a ház-ig*, as far as the house.
11. Causative: *ért*, as *pénz-ért*, for money; *barátság-ért*, for friendship.
12. Auxiliary: *val*, *vel*, as *ásó-val*, with a spade. [Note: with nouns ending in consonants *val* or *vel* drops the *v* and doubles the consonant, as *kezem-mel*, and not *kezem-vel*, with my hand.]
13. Transmuting: *vá*, *vé*, as *Lót neje só-vá változ-ott*, Lot's wife was turned into salt.
14. Demonstrative: *úl*, *ül*, as *mintá-ul küldök*, I send as a sample; *példá-ul*, for instance.

The Postposition.* (*Névutók.*)

The Hungarian language has no prepositions; it has *post*positions, for they are always put *after* the noun.

The postpositions expressing place are divided into three classes; they answer the three questions—*hol?* where? (place); *hová?* whither?; *honnan?* where from?

The postpositions answering the question *hol?* are: *alatt*, under; *előtt*, before; *mellett*, beside; *mögött*, behind; *között* or *közt*, between, amongst; *fölött* or *felett*, above; *körül*, round.

The postpositions answering the question *hová?* are: *alá*, under; *elé*, in front of; *mellé*, beside; *közé*, between, amongst; *fölé*, above; *felé*, towards, in the direction of; *köré*, round.

The postpositions answering the question *honnan?* are: *alól*, from beneath; *elől*, from the front; *mellől*, from the side; *mögül*, from behind; *közül*, from amongst; *felől*, from the side of.

* For list of postpositions see pp. 63-66.

All these postpositions take pronominal suffixes, as *alatt-am*, under me; *alatt-ad*, under thee; *alatt-a*, under him; *alatt-unk*, under us; *alatt-atok*, under you; *alatt-uk*, under them.

Körül forms *körülött-em*, *körülött-ed*, *körülötte*, etc. The other postpositions are: *után*, after; *múlva*, at the end of (does not take any suffix); *közben*, in the midst of (no suffix); *óta*, since (no suffix); *által*, by; *nélkül*, without; *szerint*, according to; *ellen*, against; *iránt*, towards; *miatt*, on account of; *végett*, because, for; *helyett*, instead; *gyanánt*, in the shape of (no suffix).

The postpositions *át*, through, above, *keresztül*, across, *innen*, on this side, *túl*, on the other side, *belül*, within, *kivül*, without, *alul*, above, *fölül*, underneath, require the suffixes *n*, *on*, *en*, *ön*, to be added to the preceding substantive.

Fogva, on account of, requires *nál*, *nél*, but when it means "since" it requires *tól*, *től*. *Képest*, in proportion to, requires *hoz*, *hez*, *höz*. *Nézve*, as to, requires, *ra*, *re*. *Együtt*, together, requires *val*, *vel*, to be added to the substantive.

The Adjective.* (*A Melléknév.*)

When the adjective is used as a substantive, all suffixes, except the possessive ones (even the article *az* or *a*) may be used with it.

A Qualificative adjective always precedes the substantive and does not change, as *a nagy asztal*, the large table; *a nagy asztalok*, the large tables.

An Attributive adjective is placed after the substantive, and takes suffixes of number. The verb in the present is not expressed: *az asztal nagy*, the table is large; *az asztalok nagyok*, the tables are large.

When a question is made the adjective is put before the substantive, as *Magas a torony?*—Is the tower high?

Adjectives are inflected in the same way as substantives, but there are the following variations from the general rule :—

Not all adjectives ending in a vowel take *k*. Those which end in *i* take *ek*, as *régi*, ancient, *régi-ek*. Those which end in *ú* or *ű* take sometimes *k*, sometimes *ak* or *ek*, as *hosszú*, long, *hosszúk* or *hosszú-ak*.

The adjectives containing one or more sharp vowels and ending with *s* (*as*, *os*, *ós*) and *ékony* take *ak*; the others take *ok*.

All the adjectives containing one or more mediate vowels take *ek*.

The suffix *ök* is not used for adjectives.

When the adjective *kis*, small, is a predicate, then it takes the form *kicsiny*.

Adjectives put in apposition precede the substantive, as Charles the Great, *Nagy Károly*.

Comparison of Adjectives.

The comparative of equality is expressed by the words *oly*, *olyan*, *éppoly*, *éppen oly*, *szintoly*, put before adjectives; "as" is translated by *mint*. Thus: *Bátyám oly nagy*, *mint te*, my brother is as tall as thou.

The negation *nem* is put before *oly*; as *Az iskola nem oly nagy*, *mint a templom*, the school is not so large as the church.

The comparative of superiority is formed by adding *bb* to adjectives ending with a vowel, *abb* or *ebb* to those ending with consonants.

* For list of adjectives see pp. 55-58. For Demonstrative Adjectives see Demonstrative Pronouns, p. 73.

Final *a* and *e* become longer when *bb* is joined to it; thus, *drága*, expensive, becomes *drágább*, more expensive, while *ó* shortens its sound in *jó*, good, *jobb*, better.

The superlative is formed by prefixing *leg* or *legesleg* to the comparative, as *legjobb*, the best.

The following adjectives are irregular in their comparatives:

	Comparative.		Comparative.
szép, beautiful	*szebb*	*nagy*, big	*nagyobb*
sok, much	*több*	*jó*, good	*jobb*
hosszú, long	*hosszabb*	*ifju*, young	*ifjabb*
könnyű, easy, light	*könnyebb*		

The superlative is regular.

The Pronoun. (*A Névmás.*)

Personal Pronouns.

They are: *én*, I; *te*, thou; *ő*, he, she; *mi*, we; *ti*, you; *ők*, they.

Singular.

N.	*én*, I	*te*, thou	*ő*, he *or* she
D.	*nekem*, to *or* for me	*neked*, to *or* for thee	*neki*, to *or* for him, her
A.	*engem*, me	*téged*, thee	*őt* or *őtet*, him, her

Plural.

N.	*mi*, we	*ti*, ye *or* you	*ők*, they
D.	*nekünk*, to *or* for us	*nektek*, to *or* for ye, you	*nekik*, to *or* for them
A.	*minket* or *bennünket*, us	*titeket* or *benneteket*, ye *or* you	*őket*, them

The second form of the accusative—*bennünket*, *benneteket*—is more emphatic, and should be translated into English: all of us, all of you, all of them.

As to attributive and genitive cases of the personal pronouns they are in the singular *nekem, neked, neki*; in the plural *nekünk, nektek, nekik.*

If the possessor is represented by a pronoun governing the object possessed directly, then the attributive pronoun is not placed before its object, which, being suffixed with the pronoun, expresses the person to whom it belongs; e.g., *kalap-om*, my hat; *kalap-od*, thy hat; *kalap-ja*, his hat.

But when an emphasis is necessary, then the uninflected personal is to be used instead of the attributive pronoun; e.g., *Az én kalapom*, my hat—not yours.

The attributive pronoun is always used in its inflected form—*nekem, neked*, etc.—when it stands as subjective and not written out at all; if it stands as attribute, then it is in its uninflected form—*én, te, ő*, etc.

Possessive Pronouns.

They are: *enyém*, mine; *tied*, thine; *övé*, his; *miénk*, ours; *tietek*, yours; *övék*, theirs.

These pronouns are a contraction of possessor and object possessed, They are formed of the personal pronoun as possessor and the suffixes of the objective case. They stand by themselves: *ez enyém*, this is mine; *enyém*, it is mine; and they take all the suffixes of the substantives except those of the plural, which they form in the same way as the personal suffixes—viz., *enyém*, *tied*, *övé*, *miénk*, *tietek*, *övék*—used when the object possessed is in the singular; *enyéim*, *tieid*, *övéi*, *mieink*, *tieitek*, *övéik*—used when the object possessed is in the plural.

These are the forms of the pronouns that would correspond to the substantives inflected with the suffixes for place or direction:—

	Singular.	Plural.
RETAINING OR REMAINING—*Ben.*		
	bennem, *benned*, *benne*	*bennünk*, *bennetek*, *bennük*
	in me, etc.	
INDICATING—*Rajt.*		
	rajtam, *rajtad*, *rajta*	*rajtunk*, *rajtatok*, *rajtuk*
	on me, etc.	
RESTING—*Nál.*		
	nálam, *nálad*, *nála*	*nálunk*, *nálatok*, *náluk*
	with me, etc.	
INWARD DIRECTION—*Be.*		
	belém, *beléd*, *belé*	*belénk*, *belétek*, *beléjük*
	into me, etc.	
UPWARD DIRECTION—*Ra.*		
	rám, *rád*, *rá*	*ránk*, *rátok*, *rájok*
	on me.	
APPROACHING—*Hoz.*		
	hozzám, *hozzád*. *hozzá*	*hozzánk*, *hozzátok*, *hozzájok*
	towards me.	
OUTWARD DIRECTION—*Bel.*		
	belőlem, *belőled*, *belőle*	*belőlünk*, *belőletek*, *belőlök*
	out of me, from me, etc.	
DOWNWARD DIRECTION—*Ró.*		
	rólam, *rólad*, *róla*	*rólunk*, *rólatok*, *róluk*
	of me, etc.	
MOVING AWAY—*Től.*		
	tőlem, *tőled*, *tőle*	*tőlünk*, *tőletek*, *tőlök*
CAUSATIVE—*Ért.*		
	értem, *érted*, *érte*	*értünk*, *értetek*, *értük*
	because of me, for me, etc.	

Reflexive Pronouns.

They are: *magam*, myself; *magad*, thyself; *maga*, himself; *magunk*, ourselves; *magatok*, yourselves; *maguk*, themselves.

Maga has also the meaning "alone"; as *magam vagyok*, I am alone. Sometimes *maga* has the meaning of "my own"; as *magam könyve*, my own book.

The other forms of *maga* are:

en magam or *ennenmagam*, myself	*minmagunk* or *minnenmagunk*
tenmagad or *tennenmagad*	*tinmagatok* or *tinnenmagatok*
önmaga or *önnönmaga*	*önmagunk* or *önnönmagunk*

NOTE.—*Másodmagammal*, I with another; *harmadmagammal*, I and two others; *negyedmagammal*, I and three others, etc.

When the relation is reciprocal, then they are reciprocals; as *egymást*, one another, each other.

Demonstrative Pronouns.[1]

They are: *ez*, this; *emez*, this here; *ugyanez*, this same; *az*, that; *amaz*, that there; *ugyanaz*, that same.

Ez and *az*, prefixed with *ugyan* or alone, point to a certain thing among others of the same class; while *ezen*, *azon*, refer to certain things among others of any class.

Az and *ez* follow the substantive and are inflected; *azon* and *ezen* stand before it and could not be inflected.

Before suffixes beginning with a consonant, *az* and *ez* change *z* into the first letter of the suffix. *Az-nak* changes into *annak*; *az-ba* changes into *abba*; *az-ra* into *arra*, etc.

The other forms (mostly obsolete) of *maga* are:

enmagam or *ennenmagam*, myself	*minmagunk*
tenmagad or *tennenmagad*	*tinmagatok*

They are: *ki*, who, *mely*, which, *mi*, what—for substantives; *minő*, *milyen*, such as—for adjectives; *ahány*, *akárhány*, *mennyi*, *amennyi*, as many as—for numerals. They are inflected like substantives.

Interrogative Pronouns.

These are, for persons: *ki?* *kicsoda?* who?; *melyik?* which? For things: *mi?* *micsoda?* what? *melyik?* which? For quality: *milyen?* *minő?* *mifele?* what kind? For the cardinal numbers: *hány?* *mennyi?* how many? and for ordinals: *hányadik?* which?—as well as the question for multiplication, *hányszor?* how many times?

The Verb.[2] (*Az Ige.*)

Before other verbs can be conjugated, it is necessary to learn the irregular verb *lenni*, to be:—

INDICATIVE MOOD.

Present Tense.	Imperfect *or* Past Tense.[3]	Present Perfect Tense.
vagyok, I am, etc.	*valék*, I was, etc.	*voltam*, I have been, etc.
vagy	*valál*	*voltál*
van	*vala*	*volt*
vagyunk	*valánk*	*voltunk*
vagytok	*valátok*	*voltatok*
vannak	*valának*	*voltak*

[1] There is no distinction between Demonstrative *Adjectives* and *Pronouns*.
[2] For list of verbs see pp. 59-63.
[3] The imperfect tense is never used now, except occasionally in poetry.

Past Perfect Tense.

voltam vala, I had been, etc.
voltál vala
volt vala
voltunk vala
voltatok vala
voltak vala

Future Tense.

leszek, I shall be, etc.
lészsz
lesz or *leszen*
leszünk
lesztek
lesznek

IMPERATIVE MOOD.

légy, be thou
legyen, be he *or* let him be
legyünk, be we *or* let us be
legyetek, be you
legyenek, be they *or* let them be

SUBJUNCTIVE MOOD.

Present Tense.

hogy legyek, that I may be, etc.
„ *légy*
„ *legyen*
„ *legyünk*
„ *legyetek*
„ *legyenek*

Past Tense.

hogy voltam légyen, that I might be, etc.
„ *voltál* „
„ *volt* „
„ *voltunk* „
„ *voltatok* „
„ *voltak* „

Future (conditional) Tense.

ha leendek, (if) I should be
„ *leendesz*
„ *leend*
ha leendünk, (if) we should be
„ *leendetek*
„ *leendenek*

CONDITIONAL MOOD.

Present Tense.

volnék I would *or* should be, etc.
volnál
volna
volnánk
volnátok
volnának

Past Tense.

voltam volna, I would *or* should have been, etc
voltál volna
volt volna
voltunk volna
voltatok volna
voltak volna

INFINITIVE MOOD.

lenni, to be.

With Personal Suffixes. In order to well understand the infinitive with the personal suffix, we add the verb *kellene*, ought.

lennem kellene, I ought to be, etc.
lenned kellene
lennie kellene
lennünk kellene, we ought to be
lennetek „
lenniök „

PARTICIPLES.

Imperfect: *való*, *levő*, *lévő*, being. Perfect: *volt*, been.
Future: *leendő*, about to be. Adverbial: *levén*, having been.
Potential form: *lehet*, may *or* can be.

The verbs are divided into Active and Medial. Then active verbs are subdivided into (*a*) Transitive and (*b*) Intransitive, while medial verbs are subdivided into (*a*) Active or deponent, (*b*) Passive, (*c*) Neuter.

Transitive and causal verbs have significant terminations; the indefinite, as *verek*, I beat (someone), and the definite, as *verem a lovat*, I beat the horse.

Conjugation of Transitive Verbs.

1st Conjugation.—*Varrni*, to sow.

INDICATIVE MOOD.

Present Tense:

Indefinite form.	Definite form.
varrok, I sow, etc.	*varrom*, I sow it, etc.
varrsz	*varrod*
varr	*varrja*
varrunk	*varrjuk*
varrtok	*varrjátok*
varrnak	*varrják*

Imperfect Tense:*

Indefinite form.	Definite form.
varrék, I sowed, etc.	*varrám*, I sowed it, etc.
varrál	*varrád*
varra	*varrá*
varránk	*varrók*
varrátok	*varrátok*
varrának	*varrák*

Present Perfect Tense:

Indefinite form.	Definite form.
varrtam, I have sown, etc.	*varrtam*, I have sown it, etc.
varrtál	*varrtad*
varrt	*varrta*
varrtunk	*varrtuk*
varrtatok	*varrtátok*
varrtak	*varrták*

The Pluperfect tense is the same as the Past tense, after which *volt* or *vala* is put:

varrtam vala (*volt*), I had sown, etc.
varrtál vala (*volt*), etc.

Future:

Indefinite form.	Definite form.
varrni fogok, I shall sow, etc.	*varrni fogom*, I shall sow it, etc.
„ *fogsz*	„ *fogod*
„ *fog*	„ *fogja*
„ *fogunk*	„ *fogjuk*
„ *fogtok*	„ *fogjátok*
„ *fognak*	„ *fogják*

IMPERATIVE MOOD.

Indefinite.	Definite.
varrj, do thou sow	*varrjad*, sow thou it
varrjon, let him sow	*varrja*, let him sow it
varrjunk, let us sow	*varrjuk*, let us sow it
varrjatok, sow (you)	*varrjátok*, you sow it
varrjanak, let them sow	*varrják*, let them sow it

* Now obsolete; see footnote 3, p. 73.

Subjunctive Mood.

Present Tense.

Indefinite.	Definite.
hogy varrjak, I may sow, etc.	*hogy varrjam*, I may sow it, etc.
,, *varrj*	,, *varrjad*
,, *varrjon*	,, *varrja*
,, *varrjunk*	,, *varrjuk*
,, *varrjatok*	,, *varrjátok*
,, *varrjanak*	,, *varrják*

Past Tense.

hogy varrtam légyen, that I might have sown, etc.

This tense is formed by putting *légyen* after the past tense of the indicative, and the conjunction *hogy* before it.

Future Tense.

ha varrandok, if I should sow	*ha varrandom*, if I should sow it
,, *varrandasz*	,, *varrandod*
,, *varrand*	,, *varrandja*
,, *varrandunk*	,, *varrandjuk*
,, *varrandotok*	,, *varrandjátok*
,, *varrandanak*	,, *varrandják*

Conditional Mood.

Present Tense.

varrnék, I might, should *or* would sow	*varrnám*, I might, should *or* would sow it
varrnál	*varrnád*
varrna	*varrná*
varrnánk	*varrnók*
varnátok	*varrnátok*
varrnának	*varrnák*

Past Tense.

varrtam volna, I should *or* would have sown	*varrtam volna*, I should *or* would have sown it
varrtál ,,	*varrtad* ,,
varrt ,, etc.	*varrta* ,, etc.

Infinitive.

varrni, to sow.

With Personal Suffixes:

Sing. *varrnom, varrnod, varrnia*. Plur. *varrnunk, varrnotok, varrniok*.

Participles.

Imperf. *varró*, sowing. Perf. *varrott*, sown. Fut. *varrandó*, to be sown.
Adverbial: *varrva, varrván*.

2nd Conjugation.—*Verni*, to beat.

Indicative Mood.

Present Tense.		Imperfect Tense.*	
Indefinite.	Definite.	Indefinite.	Definite.
(I beat, etc.)	(I beat it, etc.)	(I beat, etc.)	(I beat it, etc.)
verek	*verem*	*verék*	*verém*
versz	*vered*	*verél*	*veréd*
ver	*veri*	*vere*	*veré*
verünk	*verjük*	*verénk*	*verők*
vertek	*veritek*	*verétek*	*verétek*
vernek	*verik*	*verének*	*verék*

*See footnote 3, p. 73.

Present Perfect Tense.		Future.	
(I have beaten)	(I have beaten it)	(I shall beat)	(I shall beat it)
vertem	*vertem*	*verni fogok*	*verni fogom*
vertél	*verted*	,, *fogsz*	,, *fogod*
vert	*verte*	,, *fog*	,, *fogja*
vertünk	*vertük*	,, *fogunk*	,, *fogjuk*
vertetek	*vertétek*	,, *fogtok*	,, *fogjátok*
vertek	*verték*	,, *fognak*	,, *fogják*

Pluperfect as Past, with *volt* or *vola*.

IMPERATIVE MOOD.

Definite.	Indefinite.
verj, do thou beat	*verjed*, beat thou it
verjen, let him beat	*verje*, let him beat it
verjünk, let us beat	*verjük*, let us beat it
verjetek, beat (you)	*verjétek*, you beat it
verjenek, let them beat	*verjék*, let them beat it

SUBJUNCTIVE MOOD.

Present Indefinite.	Definite.	Future Indefinite.	Definite.
hogy verjek	*hogy verjem*	*ha verendek*	*ha verendem*
,, *verj*	,, *verjed*	,, *verendesz*	,, *verended*
,, *verjen*	,, *verje*	,, *verend*	,, *verendi*
,, *verjünk*	,, *verjük*	,, *verendünk*	,, *verendjük*
,, *verjetek*	,, *verjétek*	,, *verendetek*	,, *verenditek*
,, *verjenek*	,, *verjék*	,, *verendenek*	,, *verendik*

Past: *hogy vertem légyen*, etc.

CONDITIONAL MOOD.

Present Indefinite.	Definite.	Past Indefinite.	Definite.
vernék	*verném*	*vertem volna*	*vertem volna*
vernél	*vernéd*	*vertél* ,,	*verted* ,,
verne	*verné*	*vert* ,,	*verte* ,,
vernénk	*vernők*	*vertünk* ,,	*vertük* ,,
vernétek	*vernétek*	*vertetek* ,,	*vertétek* ,,
vernének	*vernék*	*vertek* ,,	*verték* ,,

INFINITIVE.

verni, to beat.

With Personal Pronouns:

Sing. *vernem, verned, vernie*. Plur. *vernünk, vernetek, verniök*.

PARTICIPLES.

Imperf. *verő*. Perf. *vert*. Fut. *verendő*. Adverbial: *verve, vervén*.

Medial Verbs.

They are Deponent, Passive and Neuter. Only the last two have the indefinite form. The deponents may be used in a transitive sense, and can be declined also in the definite form; e.g., *lakni* (to dwell) is neuter, *lakni* (to inhabit) is transitive, for there must be an object inhabited. In the indefinite form these are conjugated like neuter (medial), and in the definite like the active verbs; as

Indefinite: *lakom, lakol, lakik, lakunk, laktok, laknak*, I dwell, etc.
Definite: *lakom, lakod, lakja, lakjuk, lakjátok, lakják*, I inhabit (this house), etc.

In the Medial verbs the 3rd person sing. of the present tense indicative ends in *ik*; the active and intransitive and transitive verbs have no distinguishing ending. For this reason the Hungarian grammarians divide the verbs into *ikes* and *iktelen ige*; viz., verbs with *ik* and without *ik*.

Forms of the Verbs.

PRIMITIVE: *ir*, he writes.

FACTITIVE: *irat*, he causes, orders or commands to write.

FREQUENTATIVE: *irogat* indicates a repetition of the action expressed in the Primitive.

DIMINUTIVE: *irkál* (he is scribbling) signifies a playful action.

PERMISSIVE: *irhat*, he may or can write.

If the 1st person acts upon the 2nd person, the distinguishing termination of the verb will be for all moods and tenses *lak* (for flat words) or *lek* (for sharp words); e.g., *verlek*, I beat thee; *várlak*, I expect thee. But when acting upon a substantive in the 3rd person, the general rule is to be followed; e.g.,

Indefinite: *verek, versz, ver, verünk, vertek, vernek*, I beat, etc.
Definite: *verlek* or *verem, vered, veri, verjük, veritek, verik*, I beat (it) etc.

Participles.

Imperfect: *ó, ő*; e.g., *egy arató ember*, a reaping man (man that reaps)
Perfect: *t, ott, ett, ölt*; e.g., *az aratott gabona*.
Future: *andó, endő*; e.g., *az aratandó búza*, the wheat to be reaped.

The first two have adverbial forms: for the present, *va, ve*, e.g., *sétálva* walking; for past *ván, vén*, e.g., *séltálván*, having been walking.

EXAMPLES OF THE USE OF THE FIVE PARTICIPLES.

Egy szenvendő ember, a suffering man.
Egy szenvedett ember, a suffered (tolerated) man.
Egy szenvendendő ember, a man to be suffered.

Adverbial participles are not inflected, while adjective participles are inflected as adjectives and, like these, may stand for substantives; e.g., *egy szenvedő ember*, a suffering man; *egy szenvedő*, a sufferer.

The Imperfect participle is used both as adjective and substantive; e.g., *szenvedő*, sufferer, *iró*, writer, *látogató*, visitor.

Every transitive verb has two forms, the definite and the indefinits, and the chief difficulty in Hungarian is to know which form to use. The definite form is used when the object is a clearly marked-out one; the indefinite form when the object is more or less indefinite.

e.g., I am writing "this letter," *ezt a levelet* irom.
I am writing "letters," *leveleket* irok

Of active and of medial verbs (verbs at the same time active and passive) may be formed causal verbs by adding *at, tat* to flat sounding, and *et, tet* to sharp sounding verbs. The meaning of the causal verbs differs from the primitive form in that the action is not done by the agent itself, but that the latter causes something or somebody else to do it. In

English there is no corresponding form ; in German it is expressed by the infinitive and the verb *lassen*, e.g., *olvastatni* (in German, *lesen lassen*), to cause to read. All causal verbs are transitive and are conjugated in the indefinite and definite form.

Hungarian has no passive voice for active verbs, but grammarians have introduced a so-called passive voice for transitive verbs, restricted to a few of them only. The root of the passive is the same as of the causal verb, but it is conjugated like the neuter verb, as *szeretni*, to love, *olvasni* to read ; e.g.,

Indefinite.		Indefinite.		Definite.
szeret-tet-em	I am beloved, etc.	*olvas-tat-ok*	I cause to read, etc.	*olvas-tat-om*
szeret-tet-el		*olvas-tat-sz*		*olvas-tat-od*
szeret-tet-ik		*olvas-tat*		*olvas-tat-ja*
szeret-tet-ünk		*olvas-tat-unk*		*olvas-tat-juk*
szeret-tet-tek		*olvas-tat-ok*		*olvas-tat-játok*
szeret-tet-nek		*olvas-tat-nak*		*olvas-tat-ják*

Examples of Conjugations.

Indicative Mood.

Present.

1.		2.		3.	
lak-om	I dwell, etc.	*vétkez-em*	I am sinning etc.	*ütköz-öm*	I am attacking *or* encountering, etc.
lak-ol		*vétkez-el*		*ütköz-öl*	
lak-ik		*vétkez-ik*		*ütköz-ik*	
lak-unk		*vétkez-ünk*		*ütköz-ünk*	
lak-tok		*vétkez-tek*		*ütköz-tök*	
lak-nak		*vétkez-nek*		*ütköz-nek*	

Imperfect.

lak-ám	I dwelt, etc.	*vétkez-ém*	I was sinning etc.	*ütköz-ém*	I was attacking *or* encountering, etc.
lak-ál		*vétkez-él*		*ütköz-él*	
lak-ék		*vétkez-ék*		*ütköz-ék*	
lak-ánk		*vétkez-énk*		*ütköz-énk*	
lak-átok		*vétkez-étek*		*ütköz-étek*	
lak-ának		*vétkez-ének*		*ütköz-ének*	

The Past, Pluperfect and Future are the same as the indefinite of active verbs.

Subjunctive Mood.

lak-jam	*vétkez-zem*	*ütköz-zem*
lak-jál	*vétkez-zél*	*ütköz-zél*
lak-jék	*vétkez-zék*	*ütköz-zek*
lak-junk	*vétkez-zünk*	*ütköz-zünk*
lak-jatok	*vétkez-zetek*	*ütköz-zetek*
lak-janak	*vétkez-zenek*	*ütköz-zenek*

Participles.

lakó	*vétkező*	*ütköző*
lakott	*vétkezett*	*ütközött*
lakandó	*vetkezendő*	*ütközendő*
lakva	*vétkezve*	*ütközve*
lakván	*vétkezvén*	*ütközven*

Sz Mortifying Verbs.

These are verbs whose verbal roots terminate in *sz*, but which retain this *sz* only in the present tense of the indicative mood, while they drop or change it into other letters in all other cases. They are conjugated as follows:

Hinni, to believe.

INDICATIVE MOOD.

Definite.	Imperfect Indefinite.	Definite.
hisz-em, I believe (it),	*hivék*, I believed,	*hivém*
hisz-ed etc.	*hivél* etc.	*hivéd*
hisz-i	*hive*	*hivé*
hisz-szük	*hivénk*	*hivők*
hisz-itek	*hivétek*	*hivétek*
hisz-ik	*hivének*	*hivék*

Here a *v* has been put between the two vowels in place of *sz*, which was mortified, i.e., dropped.

Past Tense: *hittem*, etc.

Future Definite: *hinni fogok*, etc. Indefinite: *hinni fogom*, etc.

SUBJUNCTIVE MOOD.

Present Indefinite.		Present Definite.	
higyjek	*higyjünk*	*higyjem*	*higyjük*
higyj	*higyjetek*	*higyjed*	*higyjétek*
higyjen	*higyjenek*	*higyje*	*higyjék*

Past Indefinite: *hittem légyen*, *hittél légyen*, etc.

,, Definite: *hittem légyen*, *hitted légyen*, etc.

Future Definite: *hiendek*, etc. Indefinite: *hiendem*, etc.

CONDITIONAL MOOD.

Present Indefinite.	Definite.	Past Indefinite.	Definite.
hinnék, etc.	*hinném*, etc.	*hittem volna*	*hittem volna*
		hittél volna, etc.	*hitted volna*, etc.

INFINITIVE.

hinni.

Infinitive inflected: *hinnem*, *hinned*, *hinnie*, *hinnünk*, *hinnetek*, *hinniök.*

PARTICIPLES.

Imperfect: *hivő*. Perfect: *hitt*. Future: *hiendő*.
Adverbial: *hivén*.

Permissive verb: *hihet*, he may believe.
Factitive verb: *hitet*, he makes believe.

Impersonal Verbs.

I. Verbs which express mere action and cannot be referred to an object or person; e.g., *villámlik*, it lightens.

II. Verbs which are used in the 3rd person only, but which may relate to the 1st, 2nd or 3rd person, governing in the dative or accusative case; e.g., *illik nekem*, it is becoming for me; *engem illet*, it concerns me; *fáj nekem*, it pains me.

Defective Verbs.

I. *Nincs*, or *nincsen*, is not, has not; plural, *nincsenek*, are not, or have not.

If the agent is in the nominative case, *nincsen* is to be translated (like *van*) by the verb "to be." with the negation "not"; with the attributive case, it is to be rendered by "to have" negatived, as *nekem nincs*, I have not; *neked nincs*, thou hast not; *neki nincs*, he has not, etc.

II. *Sincs*, *sincsen*—plural, *sincsenek*—are contractions of *sem*, neither, and *nincs*, *nincsen* or *nincsenek*; e.g., *a bátyám nincs itthon*, my elder brother is not at home; *anyám sincs*, nor my mother.

Sincs follows the same rule as *nincs*.

III. *Jer*, come (thou) along! *jerünk*, let us go! *iertek*, come (you) along!

Ne, *nesze*, *nesztek*; e.g., *ne pénz*, *nesze pénz*, look, money! or here, money! (an idiomatic expression).

Compound Verbs.

These are made by prefixing to the verbs postpositions, adverbs or suffixes for place and direction, as *venni*, to take; *elvenni*, to take away; *fölvenni*, to take up; *bevenni*, to take in. The verb is inflected in the same manner as when it stands by itself.

Irregular Verbs.

These are verbs which mortify or cause the disappearance of *ss* and *gy*. There are but two verbs mortifying *gy*—*vagyon*, to be, and *megyen*, to go. *Vagyon* is not only irregular but also imperfect, for it borrows its form for the future and the imperative from *lenni*, to become. *Megyen*, to go, is only irregular in that it has two primitive forms for the present indicative, as

megyek or *menek*, I go	*megyünk* or *menünk*, we go
mégy ,, *mész*, thou goest	*mentek*, you go
megy ,, *mén*, he goes	*mennek*, they go

The 2nd and 3rd persons plural are wanting; in all other moods and tenses this verb takes *men* as its root, and is conjugated as an intransitive verb.

The Conjunction.* (*Kötőszók.*)

COPULATIVE: *és* (abbreviated *'s*), and; *is*, also; *meg*, and; *pedig*, but, yet; *mégis*, still, yet; *ismét*, again; *hogy*, that; *sem*, neither.

DISJUNCTIVE: *vagy*, or; *vagy...vagy*, either...or; *akár...akár*, whether ...or; *sem...sem*, neither...nor.

OPPOSING: *de*, *hanem*, but; *ámde*, though; *egyébiránt*, besides; *különben*, else.

EXPLANATORY: *azaz*, that is; *vagy*, or.

CAUSAL: *mivel*, *mert*, because; *minthogy*, since, as, because.

CONCESSIVE: *bár*, *ámbár*, *habár*, *noha*, *jóllehet*, although.

CONCLUSIVE: *csak*, *csakis*, *csupán*, *mindazáltal*, nevertheless, in spite of that.

* For list of conjunctions see pp. 63-66.

CONDITIONAL: *söt, inkább, sötmég.* These have no corresponding words in English, but are construed thus: *Söt szeretni fogom,* on the contrary, I shall like it.

LOCATIVE: *ott-hol,* there where; *ahonnan,* whence.

FINAL: *hát, tehát,* therefore; *egyébiránt,* otherwise; *elvégre, utoljára,* concluding, at last, finally.

The Adverb.* (*Igehatározók.*)

Hol? (where?): *itt, itten,* here; *ott, ottan,* there; *sehol,* nowhere; *máshol, másutt,* somewhere else; *valahol,* somewhere; *mindenhol, mindenütt,* everywhere. To this category belong also all substantives inflected with suffixes of place; e.g., *a házon,* upon the house; *a házban,* in the house.

Honnan? (whence?): *innen,* hence; *onnan,* thence; and substantives with suffixes, e.g., *a házról, a szobából,* etc.

Hova? (whither?): *ide,* hither; *oda,* thither; *erre,* this way; *arra,* that way; *valahová,* to somewhere.

Meddig? (to where?):

addig, as far as there
eddig, as far as here; and all nouns with *ig*
ma, to-day
holnap, to-morrow
most, mostan, now
máskor, another time
mindig, always
soha, never
azonnal, at once
este, in the evening
reggel, in the morning
nappal, in the day time
éjszaka, in the night time
az idén, this year
multkor, the other day
a multban, in the past
jövőben, in the future
időnként, yearly
igy, so (for near)
úgy, so (for distant)
emigy, in this way
amúgy, in that way
hogyan, how
hol, where
itt, here
igen, itt, yes, here

The Comparative and Superlative of adverbs are formed in the same way as in adjectives; e.g.,

Adj.: *szép* (pretty), *szebb, legszebb.*

Adv.: *szépen, szébben, légszebben.*

Adv.: *inkább* (sooner, rather), *leginkább* (soonest, especially).

The Interjection. (*Indulatszók.*)

Grief: *o! oh! jaj!* alas!
Joy: *juh!*

* For list of adverbs see pp. 63-66

Etymology.

New words are formed in two ways:

(1) By means of affixes, called formatives.
(2) By putting words together.

Those in the first class are called derivatives; in the latter, compounds.

The formatives create new ideas, as *ház*, house; *házaló*, pedlar; *házasság*, matrimony, marriage.

An inflected word cannot take a formative, but a word formed by means of a formative is inflected according to the part of speech to which it belongs. Derivatives may also take formatives.

Examples showing the stem-word of the following derivatives:

Harc (subst.), battle.
harci (adj.), pertaining to battle.
harcias (adj.), valorous, warlike
harciaskod (*-ni*) (verb), to battle, to be engaged in war.
harciaskodás (abstr. subst.), struggle, the state of being at war, challenging.
harciaskodási (adj.), pertaining to struggle, war, or fighting

Substantives are formed by adding *ság*, *ség* to adjectives, as *szép*, pretty (adj.), *szép-ség*, beauty; *jó*, good (adj.), *jó-ság*, goodness.

By adding *ás*, *és* to verbs; e.g., *áll* (*-ni*), to stand, *áll-ás*, position, standing.

By adding *as*, *es*, *ös*, or *ár*, *ér* to substantives, new substantives are formed; e.g., *asztal*, table, *asztalos*, joiner; *kés*, knife, *késes*, cutler; *kád*, coop, tub, *kádár*, cooper.

Imperfect participles can be used as substantives; e.g., *olvasó*, reader; *arató* reaper.

Diminutives are formed by adding *ka*, *ke*; e.g., *lány*, a girl, *lány-ka*, a little girl. By adding *ocska*, *ecske*; e.g., *ablak*, window, *ablak-ocska*, a small window.

Adjectives are formed by adding *as*, *os*, *es*, *ös* to substantives; e.g., *hely*, place, *helyes*, proper (in the right place); *toll*, feather, *tollas*, provided with feathers; *arany*, gold, *aranyos*, golden, or covered with gold.

Talan or *telen* are negatives; as *hely-telen*, improper; *határ-talan*, without limit.

If *i* is put after names of places it should be translated by "of," as *budapest-i*, of Budapest; *ház-i*, domestic.

Diminutives of adjectives are formed by adding *s* to adjectives ending with a vowel, or *es*, *ás*, *os*, to consonants; e.g., *sárga*, yellow, *sárgás*, yellowish; *öreg*, old, *öreges*, elderly.

Verbs are formed by adding *al*, *ol*, *el*, or *oz*, *ez*, to substantives, which then become active verbs; as *ház-al* (*-ni*), to peddle; *vas-al* (*-ni*), to iron; *ablak-oz* (*-ni*), to furnish with windows.

By adding *it*, *ül*, *ül* to adjectives—the former for transitive and the latter for intransitive verbs—as *kék*, blue; *kékít*, he makes blue; *kékül*, it is getting blue (by itself).

By adding *oz*, *őz*, *ez*, *áz* to postpositions, as *alá*, under, *aláz* (*-ni*), to humble; *túl*, beyond, *túloz* (*-ni*), to exaggerate.

As there are no genders in Hungarian, the suffix *né* (wife of) or *nő* (in the case of occupation or calling) is added to the noun to distinguish a woman from a man; e.g., *király*, king, *királyné*, queen; *szinész*, actor, *szinésznő*, actress. Queen Alexandra is a *királyné* (wife of a king); Queen Victoria was a *királynő* (queen in her own right).

To distinguish the sex of persons of the same nationality, *ember* (man) or *nő* (woman) is added, as in English, but the two words are kept separate; e.g. *angol ember*, Englishman, *angol nő*, Englishwoman.

Many of the domestic animals have separate names to distinguish their sex, as in English; e.g., *kakas*, cock, *tyúk*, hen. In every other case the name of the animal is preceded by *hím* or *kan* to denote a male, and by *nőstény* to signify a female; e.g., *hím farkas*, a he-wolf, *nőstény farkas*, a she-wolf.

Modes of address.

There are several titles in use in Hungary:—

ő felsége, his Majesty; *felséges úr*, your Majesty;
fenség, Highness.

Nagyméltóságú or *kegyelmes*, Excellency; *méltóságos*, illustrious; *nagyságos*, great, grand; *tekintetes*, distinguished, highly respected. All of these qualifications must be followed by *úr* or *uram*.

Ladies are addressed as *nagyságos asszonyom* ("great lady")—contracted *nagysád*.

Nagyságod is a title of address equivalent to "Your Honour," etc.

To translate "you" one uses *ön*, plur. *önök*; *kegyed*, plur. *kegyetek*; not very often: *maga*, plur. *maguk*.

As regards the placing of titles, *király*, king, *császár*, emperor, and *főherceg*, archduke, are always written after the proper name, as *Vilmos császár*, the Emperor William. *Herceg*, duke, *gróf*, count, and *báró*, baron, *may* be used before the name, but it is more usual to put them after it.

CONVERSATIONAL PHRASES AND SENTENCES.

Useful & Necessary Idiomatic Expressions.

(*Hasznos és szükséges nyelvjárási kifejezések és szólás módok.*)

English.	Hungarian.	Pronunciation.
If you please	*Legyen szives*	led-yen sivash
Thank you	*Köszönöm*	kĕrsĕrnĕrm
Have the goodness	*Legyen oly szives*	led-yen oy sivash
Much obliged	*Nagyon köszönöm*	nod-yon kĕrsĕrnĕrm
Yes, sir	*Igen, uram*	i-gan, ŏŏrom
No, madam	*Nem, nagysád*	nam, nodyshahd
Allow me	*Engedje meg*	an-gad-ya meg
Bring me	*Hozzon kérem*	hozzon kehrem
Do you understand?	*Érti ön?*	ehrrti ĕrn ?
Excuse me	*Bocsánatot kérek*	botchahnotot keh-rek
Give me	*Adjon kérem*	od-yon kehrem
Send me	*Küldjön nekem*	ke͡uldyĕrn nak-em
Will you tell me ?	*Mondja, kérem*	mond-yo, kehrem
Tell me [garian ?	*Mondja meg*	mond-yo meg
Do you speak Hun-	*Beszél ön magyarúl?*	bassehl ĕrn mod-yorool
Is there anyone here who speaks English ? [garian?	*Van itt valaki, aki angolúl beszél ?*	von itt voloki, oki ongolool bassehl
Can you read Hun-	*Olvas ön magyarúl?*	olvosh ĕrn mod-yorool
You read very well	*Ön jól olvas*	ĕrn yohl olvosh
How long have you learnt ?	*Mióta tanul ön ?*	miohto tonŏŏl ĕrn ?
A short time only	*Rövid idő óta*	rĕrvid id-er ohto
I find the pronunciation very difficult [accent	*A kiejtést nehéznek találom*	o ki-eytehsht na-hehznak tolahlom [sha von
You have a good	*Önnek jó kiejtése van*	ĕrnnak yoh ki-eyteh-
What do you say ?	*Mit mond ?*	mit mond ?
I have nothing to say against it	*Semmi kifogásom sincs ellene*	shemmi kifogahshom shinch allana
I beg your pardon	*Bocsánatot kérek*	botchahnotot kehrek

English.	Hungarian.	Pronunciation.
What did you ask?	*Mit kérdezett ön?*	mit kehrdazatt ěrn ?
Speak louder	*Beszéljen hangosabban*	bassehl-yen hongoshobbon
What does it signify?	*Mit jelent ez?*	mit yal-ent az ?
It does not matter	*Nem tesz semmit*	nam tess shemmit
It is all the same to me	*Nekem egyé zen mindegy*	nak-em ag-ehssan mindedy
Never mind	*Nem baj*	nam boy
What is the matter?	*Mi a baj?*	mio . boy ?
Nothing	*Semmi!*	Shemmi !
What is it about?	*Miről van szó?*	mirerl von soh ?
What is to be done?	*Mit tegyünk?*	mit ted-yeunk ?
I haven't a notion	*Fogalmam sincs róla*	fogolmom shinch rohlo
In the meantime	*Azalatt*	ozolott
Would you kindly?	*Lenne olyan jó?*	lenna oyon yoh ?
First of all	*Mindenek előtt*	mindenek alertt
That is what vexes me	*Ez boszant engem*	az bossont ang-em
He has just come in	*Éppen most jött be*	ehppan mosht yěrtt ba
Don't imagine that	*Ne képzelje azt*	ne kehpzal-ya ozt
What good is it?	*Mire jó az?*	mi-ra yoh oz ?
Where was I?	*Hol voltam?*	hol voltom ?
As for me	*A mi engem illet*	o mi ang-em illat
I cannot see any longer for me	*Én nem látok tovább*	ehn nam lahtok tovahbb
Three are enough	*Három elég nekem*	hahrom alehg nak-em
I did it in a hurry	*Sietve tettem*	shi-atva tattem
It only depends upon you	*Az öntől függ*	oz ěrnterl feugg
One is as good as the other	*Egyik olyan jó mint a másik*	ed-yik oyon yoh mint o mahshik
I can do without it	*Megleszek nélküle*	meg-lassak nehlkeula
Will you give me?	*Adna nekem?*	odno nak-em ?
Everything considered	*Mindent tekintetbe véve*	mindent takintatba vehva
I have come to tell you	*Azt jöttem mondani önnek*	ozt yěrttam mondoni ěrnnak
I am sure of it	*Biztos vagyok benne*	biztosh vod-yok banna
I don't think much of it	*Nem sokat tartok róla*	nam shokot torrtok rohlo
I can bear it no longer	*Nem tűrhetem tovább*	nam tiurr-hatem tovahbb
I like being here	*Szeretek itt lenni*	serratek itt lenni
I have been told	*Mondták nekem*	mondtahk nakem
As much as I can	*A mennyire tudom*	o mann-yi-ra töödom

English.	Hungarian.	Pronunciation.
That comes to the same thing	*Ez egyre megy*	az edyra medy
It answers the purpose	*Megfelel a célnak*	megfalal o tsehlnok
I value it very much	*Sokra becsülöm*	shokro batcheulĕrm
I am used to it	*Hozzá vagyok szokva*	hozzah vod-yok sokvo
I am not able to do it	*Nem tudom megtenni*	nam tŏŏdom megtenni
Who is it calling me	*Ki szólit engem?*	ki sohlit ang-em
It is not my fault	*Nem az én hibám*	nam oz ehn hibahm

Expressions of Emotion. (*Indulatok kifejezései.*)

(For Vocabulary see p. 26.)

What?	*Mi?*	mi?
Is it possible!	*Lehetséges?*	le-hatshehg-ash?
Indeed!	*Valóban!*	volohbon!
That is impossible	*Lehetetlen!*	le-hatatlan!
That cannot be	*Az nem lehet*	oz nam le-hat
You surprise me	*Ön meglep*	ĕrn meglap
Take care!	*Vigyázzon!*	vid-yahzzon!
I am sorry for it	*Sajnálom*	shoynahlom
I am quite vexed about it	*Boszànkodom miatta*	bossonkodom miotto
Oh! it's nothing!	*Ó, az semmi!*	oh, oz shemmi!
What a pity!	*Milyen kár!*	mi-yan kahrr!
It is a sad thing	*Szomoru dolog!*	somorrŏŏ dolog!
I am very glad	*Örvendek*	ĕrrvandek
It gives me much pleasure	*Nagy örömet szerez nekem*	nody ĕrrĕrmat serrez nakem
What a shame!	*Milyen szégyen!*	mi-yan sehd-yen!
I am ashamed of you	*Szégyenlem magamat ön miatt*	sehd-yen-lem mogomot ĕrn miott
How could you do so?	*Hogyan tehette ön?*	hod-yon te-hat-ta ĕrn?
For shame!	*Szégyelje magát!*	sehd-yal-ya mogaht
You are very much to blame	*Önt nagyon lehet hibáztatni*	ĕrnt nod-yon le-hat hibahztotni

Enquiries. (*Kérdések.*)

Do you hear me?	*Hallja amit mondok?*	holl-yo om-it mondok?
Will you kindly...?	*Lesz olyan jó hogy...*	less oyon yoh hody...?
Do you understand me?	*Érti amit mondok?*	ehrrti om-it mondok?
What is that?	*Mi az?*	mi oz?

English.	Hungarian.	Pronunciation.
What do you mean?	*Hogy érti azt?*	hody ehrrti ozt?
Are you sure?	*Biztos ön abban!*	biztosh ěrn obbon?
Can I see Mr. ... ?	*Láthatom...urat?*	laht-hot-om...ŏŏrrot?
When does he re-	*Mikor jön vissza?*	mikorr yěrn visso?
Where is...? [turn?	*Hol van...?*	hol von...?
What do you call	*Hogy hívják azt?*	hody heev-yahk ozt?
that? [mean?		
What does that	*Mit jelent az?*	mit yal-ent oz?
What is that for?	*Mire való az?*	mi-ra voloh oz?

Notices. (*Fölirások.*)

Apartments	*Kiadó szobák; kiadó*	kiodoh sobahk; kiodoh
[gentleman	*lakás [szére*	lokahsh
Bedroom for single	*Szoba egy úr ré-*	sobo edy oorr rehsehra
Entrance	*Bemenet*	bamenat
Exit	*Kijárat*	ki-yahrot
Furnished rooms	*Butorozott szobák*	bŏŏtorozott sobahk
Unfurnished rooms	*Butorozatlan szoba*	bŏŏtorozotlon sobo
Just published	*Éppen most jelent*	ehppan mosht yal-ent
Knock	*Kopogjon [meg*	kopog-yon [meg
Notice	*Felirat; értesítés*	fal-i-rot; ehrrtashee-
No admittance	*Tilos a bemenet*	tilosh o bamenat [tehsh
Please do not touch	*Ne tessék hozzá-*	ne tash-shehk hozzah-
[shoes	*nyulni [rölni*	nyŏŏlni [latěrěrlni
Please wipe your	*Tessék a cipőt letö-*	tash-shehk o tsipert
Private	*Tilos a bemenet*	tilosh o bamenat
Public notice	*Hirdetmény*	hirrdatmehny
Pull; push	*Húzza; taszítsa*	hoozzo; tosseetsho
Refreshments	*Étterem*	ehtterrem
Ring	*Csengessen*	chan-gash-shen

The Railway. (*Vaspálya.*)

(For Vocabulary see p. 36)

To the...station	*Az állomáshoz*	oz ahllomahsh-hoz
Here is my luggage	*Itt a podgyászom*	itt o pod-dyahsom
[room?		
Take it to the cloak-	*Tegye a ruha-tárba*	ted-ya o rŏŏbo-tahrrbo
I wish to register	*A podgyászt ajánlva*	o pod-dyahst oyahnlvo
my luggage for...	*szeretném feladni*	serratnehm falodni
The luggage is over	*A podgyásznak túl-*	o pod dyahsnok tool-
weight	*súlya van*	shoo-yo von

English.	Hungarian.	Pronunciation.
Get my luggage; here is the ticket	*Adja ki a podgyászomat, itt a felvételi jegy*	od-yo ki o poddyahsomot itt o falvehtali yady
Where is the waiting-room?	*Hol van a váróterem?*	hol von o vahrohterrem?
— booking-office?	*— — a pénztár?*	— — o pehnztahrr?
— refreshment-room?	*— — az állomási vendéglő?*	— — oz ahllomahshi vandehgler?
— train for ...?	*— — a vonat...felé?*	— — o vonot...faleh?
— the lavatory?	*— — az árnyékszék?*	— — oz ahrrnyehkselık?
Are you going by the express?	*Gyorsvonattal megy?*	dyorshvonottol medy?
Show me a time-table	*Mutassa a menetrendet*	mŏŏtoshsho o menatrendet
When does the train start?	*Mikor indul a vonat?*	mikorr indŏŏl o vonot?
Can I book through to N.?	*Válthatok jegyet egyenesen N. be?*	vahlt-hotok yad-yet ed-yan-eshan N. ba
I want a first-class ticket to N.	*Adjon elsőosztályú jegyet N. be?*	od-yon alsher-ostah-yoo yad-yet N. ba
How much is it?	*Mennyibe kerül?*	mann-yi-ba kerrēūl?
We want a sleeping carriage	*Háló kocsit kivánunk*	hahloh kotchit kivahnŏŏnk
— a corridor carriage	*Átjáró kocsi —*	ahtyahroh kotchi —
— family tickets	*Családjegy —*	cholahd-yady —
— a carriage for ladies	*Női szakasz —*	neri sokoss —
— a non-smoking compartment	*Nem dohányzó szakasz —*	nam do-hahnyzoh sokoss —
Is this the train for N.?	*Ez a vonat megy N. felé?*	az o vonot medy N. faleh?
Do I change anywhere on the journey?	*Át kell szállni valahol az uton?*	aht kal sahllni volohol oz ŏŏton?
Where must I change for N.?	*Hol kell átszállni N. felé?*	hol kal ahtsahllni N. faleh?
The train is just going to start	*A vonat éppen indul*	o vonot ehppan indŏŏl
Is this seat engaged?	*El van ez a hely foglalva?*	al von az o hey foglolvo?
There is no room	*Itt nincs hely*	itt ninch hey

English.	Hungarian.	Pronunciation.
Call the guard	*Hívja a kalauzt*	heev-yo o kolo-ŏŏzt
Open the door	*Nyissa ki az ajtót*	nyishsho ki oz oytoht
— the window	*– – az ablakot*	– – oz oblokot
Here is a station	*Itt az állomás*	itt oz ahllomahsh
Do we stop here?	*Megállunk itt?*	meg ahllŏŏnk itt?
Do we alight here?	*Kiszállunk itt?*	kisahllŏŏk itt?
Do we change carriages here?	*Más kocsiba szállunk itt?*	mahsh kotchibo sahllŏŏnk itt?
Five minutes	*Öt perc*	ĕrt perrts
The luggage train	*Podgyászvonat*	podd-yahss vonot
Send this by fast train	*Küldje ezt gyorsvonattal*	keu͡ld-ya azt dyorrshvonottol
— by slow train	*– – tehervonattal*	– – te-herr-vonottol
My luggage is lost	*Elvesztettem a podgyászomat*	alvastattam o poddyahssomot
Give me your ticket	*Adja ide a jegyét*	od-yo id-a o yad-yeht
Here it is	*Itt van*	itt von

The Steamboat. (*A gőzhajó.*)

(For Vocabulary see p. 37.)

When do we start?	*Mikor indulunk?*	mikorr indŏŏlŏŏnk?
When shall we arrive?	*Mikor érkezünk meg?*	mikorr ehrrkazeu͡nk meg?
Time is up!	*Az idő elmult*	oz id-er almŏŏlt
Wait for me!	*Várjon reám!*	vahrr-yon re-ahm!
Where is your luggage?	*Hol van a podgyásza?*	hol von o podd-yahsso?
Let us go down into the cabin	*Menjünk le a kabinba!*	men-yeu͡nk la o kobinbo
Where is my berth?	*Hol az én kabinom?*	hol oz ehn kobinom?
I want a cabin to myself	*Külön kabint szeretnék mimat*	keu͡lĕrn kobint serratnehk mimot
Look for my things	*Keresse meg a hol-*	kerrash-sha meg o hol-
There was another trunk	*Egy másik bőröndöm is volt*	edy mahshik berrĕrndĕrm ish volt
Passengers are requested to keep clear of the gangway	*Az utasok kéretnek az utat szabadon hagyni*	oz ŏŏtoshok kehratnak oz ŏŏtot sobodon hodyni

At the Custom-house. (*A vámházban.*)

(For Vocabulary see p. 36.)

English.	Hungarian.	Pronunciation.
Come to the Custom-house	*Jöjjön a vámházhoz*	yery-yĕrn o vahmhahzhoz
The Custom-house officer	*A vámházi hivatalnok*	o vahmhahzi hivotolnok
Have you your passport ?	*Megvan az utlevele ?*	megvon oz ŏŏtlavala ?
Will you examine this trunk ?	*Meg akarja vizsgálni ezt a böröndöt ?*	meg okorr-yo vizhgahlni azt o berrĕrndĕrt ?
Here are the keys	*Itt vannak a kulcsok*	itt vonnok o kŏŏlchok
Open it	*Nyissa ki*	nyish-sho ki
Unlock this box	*Nyissa ki a ládát*	nyish-sho ki o lahdaht
Have you anything to declare ?	*Van elvámolni valója ?*	von alvahmolni volohyo ?
I have nothing liable to duty	*Nincs elvámolni valóm*	ninch alvahmolni volohm
Have you any tobacco or cigars ?	*Van önnél dohány vagy szivar ?*	von ĕrnnehl do-hahny vody sivorr ?
I have a few cigars	*Néhány szivar van nálam*	neh-hahny sivorr von nahlom
Those are free	*Az vámmentes*	oz vahmmantash
Is that all ?	*Ennyi az egész ?*	ann-yi oz ag-ehss ?
What is the duty ?	*Mi a vám reá ?*	mi o vahm re-ah ?
Is my luggage passed ?	*Meg van vizsgálva a podgyászom ?*	meg von vizhgahlvo o podd-yahsom ?

Arrival. (*Megérkezés.*)

(For Vocabulary see p. 36.)

English.	Hungarian.	Pronunciation.
Call a cab	*Hozzon kocsit*	hozzon kotchit
Closed, open	*Zárt, nyitott*	zahrrt, nyitott
Put my luggage in the cab	*Tegye a podgyászomat a kocsiba*	ted-ya o podd-yahsomot o kotchibo
Cabman	*Kocsis*	kotchish
Drive me to ...	*Vigyen engem...*	vid-yen ang-em...
What is the fare by the journey ?	*Mennyit kell fizetnem árszabály szerint ?*	menn-yit kal fizatnem ahrrsobah-y' serrint?
By the hour	*Egy órára*	edy ohrahro
Drive quickly	*Hajtson gyorsan !*	hoytshon dyorrshon
Drive slower	*Hajtson lassabban !*	hoytshon loshshobbon

English.	Hungarian.	Pronunciation.
Stop! Go on!	*Álljon meg! Menjen!*	ahllyon meg! menyen!
The omnibus station	*Társaskocsi állomás*	tarrshosh-kotchi ahllomahsh
Conductor	*Vezető*	vazater
Give me a ticket	*Adjon jegyet*	od-yon yad-yet
Inside	*Belül, benn*	baleul, bann
Outside	*Künn*	keunn
Tickets please!	*Kérem a jegyet!*	kehrem o yad-yet
Full	*Megtelt*	megtalt

The Hotel. (*A szálló.*)

(For Vocabulary see p. 29.)

English	Hungarian	Pronunciation
Which is the best hotel?	*Melyik a legjobb szálló?*	meyik o lag-yobb sahlloh?
Let us have supper soon	*Vacsorázzunk hamar*	votchorahzzŏŏnk hommorr
Are our rooms ready?	*Rendben vannak a szobák?*	rendban vonnok o sobahk?
I want a bed-room	*Adjon kérem egy hálószobát*	od-yon kehrem edy hahlohsobaht
Let me see the room	*Szeretném a szobát látni*	sa-rat-nehm o sobaht lahtni
What is the price of this room?	*Mi az ára ennek a szobának?*	mi oz ahrro annak o sobahnok?
That is too dear	*Az nagyon drága*	oz nod-yon drahgo
I want a cheaper one	*Olcsóbbat szeretnék*	olchohbbot saratnehk
Have you a double-bedded room?	*Van kétágyas szoba?*	von kehtahd-yosh sobo?
Are there any letters for me?	*Jöttek leveleim?*	yĕrttak lav-al-a-im?
Where is the w.c.?	*Hol van az árnyékszék?*	hol von oz ahrrn-yehksehk?
Give me the key of my room	*Adjon a szobámhoz kulcsot*	od-yon o sobahmhoz kŏŏlchot
Can I have a warm bath?	*Kaphatok meleg fürdőt?*	kop-hotok malag feurrdert
Bring me some warm water	*Hozzon meleg vizet*	hozzon, malag vizat

Breakfast. (*Reggeli.*)

(For Vocabularies see pp. 14—19, 29—31.)

English	Hungarian	Pronunciation
Is breakfast ready?	*Kész a reggeli?*	kehss o raggeli?
Breakfast is ready	*A reggeli kész*	o raggeli kehss
Is the tea made?	*Kész a tea?*	kehss o te-o?
Some rolls	*Zsemle*	zhamla

English.	Hungarian.	Pronunciation.
Do you drink tea or coffee ?	*Teát vagy kávét iszik ön?*	te-aht vody kahveht issik ěrn ?
Sugar, cream, or milk ?	*Cukrot, tejszint, vagy tejet?*	tsöökrot, teysint, vody teyat ?
Will you take an egg ?	*Tetszik egy tojás ?*	tatsik edy toyahsh ?
These eggs are hard	*Ezek a tojások kemények*	azek o toyahshok kamehn-yak
Give me the salt, pepper, mustard	*Adjon sót, borsot, mustárt*	od-yon shoht, borrshot, mööshtahrrt
Pass me the butter	*Nyujtsa ide a vajat*	nyuytsho id-a o voyot
This butter is not fresh	*Ez a vaj nem friss*	az o voy nam frish
Bring some more	*Hozzon még*	hozzon mehg
Is the coffee strong enough ?	*Elég erős a kávé ?*	alehg a-rersh o kahveh?
We want more cups	*Nekünk több csésze kell*	nakeünk těrbb chehsa kal
Take some more sugar	*Vegyen még cukrot*	ved-yen mehg tsöökrot
A piece of toast, please	*Pirított kenyeret kérek*	pirreetott kenyerrat kehrrek
Cold meat	*Hideg hús*	hidag hoosh
A rasher of bacon	*Szalonna szelet*	solonno salat

Dinner. (*Ebéd.*)

(For Vocabularies see pages 14—19, 29—31.)

English.	Hungarian.	Pronunciation.
Give me (show me) the bill-of-fare	*Adja (mutassa) kérem az étlapot*	od-yo (möötoshsho) kehrem oz ehtlopot
What have you ready ?	*Mi van készen ?*	mi von kehssan ?
What soup will you have ?	*Milyen leves tetszik ?*	mi-yan lavash tatsik ?
Gravy soup	*Húsleves*	hooshlavash
Have you any roast beef?	*Van marhasült ?*	von morr-hosheült ?
We shall dine at six o'clock	*Hat órakor fogunk ebédelni*	hot ohrrokorr fogöönk abehdalni
Be punctual	*Legyen pontos !*	led-yen pontosh !
Are you hungry ?	*Éhes ön ?*	eh-hash ěrn ?
I am hungry	*Éhes vagyok*	eh-hash vod-yok
Are you thirsty ?	*Szomjas ön ?*	som-yosh ěrn ?
I am very thirsty	*Nagyon szomjas vagyok*	nod-yon som-yosh vod-yok
What shall I help you to ?	*Mivel szolgálhatok ?*	mival solgahl-hotok ?
Will you take some soup?	*Tetszik leves ?*	tatsik lavash ?

English.	Hungarian.	Pronunciation.
No, thank you	*Nem, köszönöm*	nam, kĕrsĕrnĕrm
Help yourself	*Szolgálja ki magát*	solgahl-yo ki mogaht
Well-done	*Jól megsülve*	yohl megshe͡ulva
Under-done	*Félig sülve*	fehlig she͡ulva
It is excellent	*Kitunő!*	kite͡uner!
Red pepper	*Paprika*	popriko
Peas	*Borsó*	borrshoh
Here is spinach	*Ez itt paraj*	az itt porroy
Cauliflower	*Karfiól*	korrfiohl
Artichokes	*Articsóka*	orrtichohko
Potatoes	*Burgonya*	bŏŏrgonyo
The mustard pot	*A mustártartó*	o mŏŏshtahrr-torrtoh
Change the plates	*Váltson tányért*	vahltshon tahn-yehrt
Give me a clean fork	*Adjon egy tiszta villát, kérem*	od-yon edy tisto villaht, kehrem
A clean knife	*Egy tiszta kést*	edy tisto kehsht
Bring me a glass of water	*Hozzon egy pohár vizet*	hozzon edy po-hahrr vizat
Give me something to drink	*Adjon kérem valamit inni*	od-yon kehrem volomit inni
What wine will you have?	*Milyen bor tetszik?*	mi-yan borr tatsik?
Here is the list	*Itt a borjegyzék*	itt o borr-yadyzehk
This wine tastes of the cork	*Ennek a bornak dugó ize van*	annak o borrnok dŏŏgoh iza von

Tea. (*Tea.*)

(For Vocabularies see pages 14—19, 29—31.)

English	Hungarian	Pronunciation
Tea is ready	*A tea kész*	o te-o kehss
Pour out the tea	*Töltse ki a teát*	tĕrltsha ki o te-aht
Bring a saucer	*Hozzon egy csésze aljat*	hozzon edy chehso ol-yot
Ring, if you please	*Csöngessen, kérem*	chĕrngashshen, kehrem
A little more milk	*Még egy kis tejet kérek*	mehg edy kish teyat kehrek
More bread	*Több kenyeret kérek*	tĕrbb ken-yerrat kehrek
Some bread and butter, some eggs	*Vajat, kenyeret és tojást kérek*	voyot, ken-yerrat ehsh toyahsht kehrek

Health. (*Egészség.*)

(For Vocabulary see p. 28.)

English.	Hungarian.	Pronunciation.
How are you ?	*Hogyan érzi magát?*	hod-yon ehrrzi mogaht?
I am very well	*Jól érzem magamat*	yohl ehrrzem mogomot
— ill	*Beteg vagyok*	batag vod-yok
— not very well	*Nem érzem magamat jól*	nam ehrrzem mogomot yohl
I hope you will soon be better	*Remélem hogy nemsokára jobban lesz*	ramehlem hody namshokahro yobbon less
Do you sleep well ?	*Jól aludt ?*	yohl olöödt ?
Pretty well, thank you	*Elég jól, köszönöm*	alehg yohl, kĕrsĕrnĕrm
I have a headache	*A fejem fáj*	o feyam fah-y'
I have caught a chill	*Meghűtöttem magamat*	meg-hīutĕrttam mogomot
I feel sick	*Rosszul érzem magamat*	rossööl ehrrzem mogomot
Send for a doctor	*Küldjön orvosért*	ke͡uld-yĕrn orrvoshehrt
She has a cough	*Köhögése van*	kĕrhĕrgehsha von
Where is there a chemist's shop ?	*Hol van itt gyógyszertár ?*	hol von itt dyohdyserrtahrr ?
How much is the doctor's fee for a visit ?	*Mennyit kell adni az orvosnak egy látogatásért ?*	mann-yit kal odni oz orrvoshnok edy lahtogotahshehrt ?
Have this prescription made up	*Ezt a receptet készítse el*	azt o ratsaptet kehseettsha al
Shake the bottle	*Az üveget fel kell rázni*	oz e͡uvag-et fal kal rahzni
Poison !	*Méreg !*	mehreg !
To be taken after each meal	*Ezt vegye be minden étkezés után*	azt ved-ya ba minden ehtkezehsh öötahn

In Town. (*A városban.*)

(For Vocabulary see p. 22.)

English.	Hungarian.	Pronunciation.
Where shall we go ?	*Hova menjünk ?*	hovvó men-ye͡unk ?
Which is the way to...?	*Merre kell menni az...?*	merra kal menni oz...?
Where does this road lead ?	*Hova vezet ez az út?*	hovvo vazat az oz oot ?
Straight before you	*Egyenesen*	ed-yanashan
To the right, left	*Jobbra, balra*	yobbro, bolro
Go up the street	*Menjen végig az utczán*	men-yen vehgig oz öötsahn
Is it far from here ?	*Messze van innen ?*	massa von innan

English.	Hungarian.	Pronunciation.
How far is it to...?	*Milyen messze van innen?* [*föld*	mi-yan massa von in-nan? [mehrtfĕrld
About a mile	*Körülbelül egy mért-*	kĕrreūl-baleūl edy
Where can I get an omnibus to...?	*Hol kaphatok omni-buszt az...?*	hol kop-hotok omni-bŏŏst oz...?
Go quickly	*Menjen gyorsan*	men-yen dyorrshon
Go slowly	*Menjen lassan*	men-yen loshshon
Straight on	*Egyenesen előre*	ed-yanashan alerra
Let us go	*Menjünk!*	men-yeūnk
Upon the outside	*Kivül*	kiveūl [ootot
Show me the way	*Mutassa meg az útat*	mŏŏtoshsho meg oz
Turn to the right	*Forduljon jobbra*	forrdŏŏl-yon yobbro
Keep to the left	*Tartson balra*	torrtshon bolro
Second turning to the right	*A második forduló jobbra*	o mahshodik forrdŏŏloh yobbro
Cross the road	*Menjen át az úton*	men-yen aht oz ooton
In what street is...?	*Melyik utcában van?*	meyik ŏŏtsahbon von...?
Is this the way to...? [F.?	*Ez az út vezet...felé?*	az oz oot vazat...faleh?
Do you know Mr.	*Ismeri ön F. urat?*	ishmerri ĕrn F. ŏŏrot?
I don't know any-one of that name	*Nem ismerek ilyen nevü urat*	nam ishmerrek i-yan naveū ŏŏrot
He is a friend of mine [well	*Barátom*	borrahtom
I know him very	*Nagyon jól ismerem*	nod-yon yohl ishmerrem
Where does he live?	*Hol lakik?*	hol lok-ik?
Close by	*Egészen közel*	ag-ehssan kĕrzal
Can you direct me to his house?	*Megmutathatná, hol van a háza?*	megmŏŏtot-hotnah, hol von o hahzo?
Is Mr. N., Mrs. N., at home?	*Itthon van N. úr? itthon van N. né*	itt-hon von N. oorr? itt-hon von N. neh os-
Good morning	*Jó reggelt* [*asszony?*	yoh reg-galt [sony?
How do you do?	*Hogy érzi magát?*	hody ehrrzi mogaht?
Very well	*Nagyon jól*	nod-yon yohl
I must go	*Mennem kell*	mennem kal
I wish you good morning	*Jó reggelt kivánok*	yoh reg-galt kivahnok
Good evening!	*Jó estét!*	yoh ashteht!
Good night!	*Jó éjszakát!*	yoh eysokaht!
Good-bye!	*Viszontlátásra!*	vissontlahtahshro!
Farewell!	*Isten önnel*	ishtan ĕrnnal

Shopping. (*Vásárlás közben.*)

(For Vocabularies see pages 14—19, 20—36, 46.)

English.	Hungarian.	Pronunciation.
How much?	*Mennyibe kerül?*	mann-yi-ba kerre͡ul?
That is too much	*Az drága*	oz drahgo
Show me some...	*Mutasson néhányat*	mŏŏ'toshshon neh-hahn- [yot...
What is the price?	*Mi az ára?*	mi oz ahrro?
Will you send them at once?	*Elküldi mindjárt?*	alke͡uldi mind-yahrrt?
I wish to buy	*Venni akarok*	venni okorrok
I will take this	*Ezt veszem*	azt vessem
Send them to...	*Küldje ezt...hez*	ke͡uld-ya azt...haz
I want some calico	*Perkál szövetet szeretnék*	perrkahl sĕrvatet serr-atnehk
I should like to see [some ribbon	*Mutasson szallago-* [*kat*	mŏŏtoshshon sollogok- [ot
This colour is too dark, light	*Ez a szín nagyon sötét, világos*	az o seen nod-yon shĕrteht, vilahgosh
Have you any narrower?	*Van valamivel keskenyebb is?*	von volomival kashkenyabb ish?
Broader?	*Szélesebb?*	sehleshabb?
What is this a yard?	*Hogy ebből egy rőf?*	hody abberl edy rerf?
It is faded	*Ez kifakult*	az kifokŏŏlt
Show me some linen	*Mutasson nekem vásznat*	mŏŏtoshshon nak-em vahssnot
Not so fine	*Nem oly finomat*	nam oy finomot
This will do	*Ez megfelel*	az megfalal
Sewing-silk	*Varró selyem*	vorroh sheyem
A skein	*Egy köteg*	edy kĕrtag
Pins; needles	*Gombostű; varrótű*	gomboshtĭu; vorrohtĭu
Mixed pins	*Vegyes gombostű*	ved-yesh gomboshtĭu
Tape	*Kötőszalag*	kĕrtersolog
A bodkin	*Zsákvarró tű*	zhahkvorroh tĭu
Show me some gloves [pair?	*Mutasson néhány keztyüt* [*pár?*	mŏŏtoshshon neh-hahny kazt-ye͡ut [pahrr?
What are they a	*Mennyibe kerül egy*	mann-yi-ba kerre͡ul edy
It is too dear	*Nagyon drága*	nod-yon drahgo
Show me some others	*Mutasson másféléket*	mŏŏtoshshon mahsh-fehlehkat
Try on these	*Próbálja föl ezeket*	prohbahl-yo fĕrl azekat
They fit you very well	*Ezek éppen jók önnek*	azek ehppan yohk ĕrn-nak

English.	Hungarian.	Pronunciation.
I will take them with me	*Ezeket magammal viszem*	az-ek-at mogommol vissem
Send all this home directly	*Küldje ezeket azonnal haza*	keūld ya az-ek-at ozonnol hoz-o
The bill, please	*Kérem a számlát*	kehrem o sahmlaht

The Dressmaker. (*A varrónő.*)

(For Vocabulary see p. 51.)

English.	Hungarian.	Pronunciation.
Here is the dressmaker	*Itt a varrónő*	itt ó vorrohner
Ask her to wait	*Kérje meg, hogy várjon*	kehrr-ya meg, hody vahrr-yon
Show her in	*Vezesse be*	vazashsha ba
Have you brought my dress?	*Elhozta a ruhámat?*	alhozto o rŏŏhahmot?
Here it is, madam	*Itt van, nagysád*	itt von, nodyshahd
Will you try it on?	*Föl tetszik próbálni?*	fěrl tatsik prohbahlni?
It fits you very well	*Nagyon jól áll*	nod-yon yohl ahll
It is not a good fit	*Nem jól áll*	nam yohl ahll
The skirt is too narrow	*Az alj nagyon szűk*	oz ol-y' nod-yon sīuk
It is too short-waisted	*A dereka nagyon rövid*	o derreko nod-yon rĕrvid
The sleeves are not wide enough	*Az ujja nem elég bő*	oz ŏŏy-yo nam al-ehg ber
Make all these alterations	*Végezze el ezeket a javításokat*	vehgazza al azekat o yoveetahshokot
What trimming would you put on?	*Milyen díszt tegyünk reá?*	mi-yan dist ted-yeūnk re-ah?
Pale pink ribbon	*Halvány rózsaszín szalagot*	holvahny rohzhoseen sologot
When can you let me have it?	*Mikor kaphatom meg?*	mikorr kop-hotom meg?
You shall have it on Saturday	*Szombaton itt lesz*	somboton itt less
Without fail	*Minden bizonnyal*	minden bizonn-yol

The Shoemaker. (*A cipész.*)

English.	Hungarian.	Pronunciation.
I wish to see some ladies' boots	*Női cipőt szeretnék látni*	neri tsipert sa-ratnehk lahtni
Take my measure	*Kérem, vegyen mértéket*	kehrem, ved-yen mehrrtehkst
The soles are rather thick	*A talp nagyon vastag*	o tolp nod-yon voshtog
They are too tight	*Nagyon szűk*	nod-yon sīuk

English.	Hungarian.	Pronunciation.
I cannot get my foot in	*Nem megy bele a lábam*	nam medy bal-a o lab bom
Here is a shoe-horn	*Itt a cipőhuzó*	itt o tsiperhöözoh
Are they comfortable? [them	*Kényelmes?* [*járni*	kehn-yal-mash? [yahrrni
I cannot walk in	*Nem tudok benne*	nam töödok banna
They hurt my heel	*Szorítja a sarkamat*	soreet-yo o shorrkomot
I must have them as soon as possible	*Minél előbb szeretném megkapni*	minehl alerbb sa-rat-nehm megkopni
I want some boot-laces [a pair?	*Cipőkötőt szeretnék* [*ja?*	tsiperkërtert sa-rat-nehk [pahrr-yo?
How much are they	*Mennyibe kerül pár-*	mann-yi-ba kerreül
I want these shoes soled and heeled	*Ezt a pár cipőt szeretném megtalpaltatni és megsarkaltatni*	azt o pahrr tsipert sa-rat-nehm megtolpoltoni ehsh megshorrkoltotni
Send my boots to be mended [done?	*Küldje el cipőmet kijavíttatni*	keüld-ya al tsipermat ki-yoveetottni
When will they be	*Mikor lesz készen?*	mikorr less kehssen?

The Laundress. (*A mosónő.*)

(For Washing List see p. 33.)

This is too limp	*Ez nagyon puha*	az nod-yon pöö-ho
You don't put enough starch in	*Nem használ elég keményitőt*	nam hossnahl al-ehg kamehn-yitert
I miss a collar	*Hiányzik egy gallér*	hiahnyzik edy gollehrr
See how badly that is done [back	*Nézze milyen rosszul van ez mosva*	nehzza mi-yan rossööl von az moshvo
You must take it	*Vigye ezt vissza* [*va*	vid-ya azt visso
This is badly ironed	*Ez rosszul van vasal-*	az rossööl von vosholvo
You have scorched this dress	*Ezt a ruhát megégette*	azt o rööhaht meg-eh-gatta
You put too much blue in my linen	*Sok kékitőt tesz a fehérnemübe*	shok kehkitert tess o fa-hehrr-nameü-ba
This is not my handkerchief	*Ez nem az én zsebkendőm*	az nam oz ehn zhab-kanderm
You have torn this dress	*Ön elszakította ezt a ruhát*	ërn alsokeetotto azt o rööhaht
Have you your bill?	*Elhozta a számlát?*	al-hozto o sahmlaht?
I want this linen washed	*Ezt a fehérnemüt ki-akarom mosatni*	azt o fa-hehrr-nameüt ki-okorrom moshotni

English.	Hungarian.	Pronunciation.
When can I have it?	*Mikor kaphatom meg?*	mikorr kop-hotom meg?
Please return this linen on ...	*Kérem küldje ezt a fehérnemüt...vissza*	kehrem keu͡ld-ya azt o fa-hehrrnameu͡t...visso
I will pay you	*Kifizetem önt*	kifizatam ĕrnt
You must bring back this list	*Hozza vissza ezt a jegyzéket*	hozzo visso azt o yadyzehket

Amusements. (*Szórakozások.*)

(For Vocabulary see p. 39.)

What is on at the...	*Mit adnak a...ban?*	mit odnok o...bon?
Shall we go?	*Elmenjünk?*	al-men-yeu͡nk?
Where can we book seats?	*Hol válthatunk jegyet?*	hol vahlt-hotŏŏnk yadyet?
Is the box-office open?	*Nyitva van a pénztár?*	nyitvo von o pehnztahr?
I should like to see a plan	*Szeretnék egy színházi tervrajzot látni*	sa-ratnehk edy seenhahzi terv-royzot lahtni
Let us take a box	*Vegyünk páholyt*	ved-yeu͡nk pah-hoyt
These seats are reserved	*Ezek a helyek le vannak foglalva*	azek o heyak la vonnok foglolvo
We will take them	*Ezeket lefoglalom*	azekat lafoglolom
Where are your seats?	*Hol van az önök helye?*	hol von oz ĕrnĕrk heya?
Where is the cloak-room?	*Hol van a ruhatár?*	hol von o rŏŏhotahr?
Who is on the stage?	*Ki van a színpadon?*	ki von o seenpodon?
Give me a programme	*Adjon egy színlapot*	od-yon edy seenlopot
What is the play?	*Mit adnak?*	mit odnok
How well the band plays!	*Milyen jól játszik a zenekar!*	mi-yan yohl yahtsik o zanakorr
Who is the conductor?	*Ki a karmester?*	ki o korrmashterr?
There is a fine orchestra	*Nagyon jó zenekar*	nod-yon yoh zan-ak-orr
What an excellent pianist!	*Milyen kitünő zongara művész!*	mi-yan kiteu͡ner zongorro mĭuvehss
An interval of fifteen minutes	*Tizenöt percnyi szünet*	tizenĕrt perrtsnyi seu͡nat
Would you like any refreshment?	*Akar valami frissítőt?*	okor volomi frish-sheetert?
Shall we go to the buffet?	*Kimenjünk az étterembe?*	kimen-yeu͡nk oz eht-taremba?

English.	Hungarian.	Pronunciation.
Is there a good museum ?	*Van itt jó muzeum?*	von itt yoh mŏŏzeŏŏm ?
The works of art are very fine	*A müvek nagyon szépek*	o mïuvak nod-yon seh-pak
Are tickets required ?	*Kell oda jegy ?*	kal od-o yady ?
How much will it [cost ?	*Mennyibe kerül ?*	mann-yi-ba kerre͡ul ?
Who sells them ?	*Hol adják ?*	hol od-yahk ?
It will take all day	*Egész napba kerül ezt megnézni*	ag-ehss nopbo kerre͡ul azt megnehzni
Then we must take some refreshment	*Akkor valami frissítő lesz szükséges*	okkor volomi frish-sheeter less se͡uksheng-esh
Can you put us up some refreshment?	*Adhat velünk valami ennivalót az útra?*	od-hot vale͡unk volomi ennivoloht oz ootro ?
Is there a good place for lunch ?	*Van itt jó ebédelő hely ?*	von itt yoh abehdaler hey ?
When does the performance begin ?	*Mikor kezdődik az előadás ?*	mikorr kazderdik oz alerodahsh ?
What time do the doors open ?	*Mikor nyitják ki az ajtókat ?*	mikorr nyityahk ki oz oytohkot ?

Cycling. (*Kerékpár.*)

(For Vocabulary see p. 42.)

I want my machine	*A gépemet szeretném*	o gehpamat sa-ratnehm
Fitted with all ac-[cessories	*Teljesen fölszerelve*	tal-yashan fĕrlserrelva
I wish to hire a...	*Bérelni akarok egy...*	behralni okorrok edy...
By the hour	*Óra számra*	ohro sahmro
By the day	*Egy napra*	edy nopro
What are your [terms ?	*Mi az ára ?*	mi oz ahro ?
Have you a cycle shelter ?	*Van itt kerékpár istálló ?*	von itt kerehkpahrr ishtahlloh ?
To tighten a nut	*A csavarzárat megszorítani*	o chovorrzahrot megsorreetoni
To loosen a nut	*A csavarzárat lazí-[tani*	o chovorrzahrot lozee-[toni
Are the roads good (bad) ?	*Jók (rosszak) az utak ?*	yohk (rossok) oz ŏŏtok?
The chain is off	*Leesett a láncz*	le-ashett o lahnts
I must pump up my tyres	*Fel kell fújni a gummi csövet*	fal kal fooyni o gŏŏmmi chĕrvat
I have broken a ...	*Eltörtem a...*	altĕrrtam o...

English.	Hungarian.	Pronunciation.
Are you ready?	*Készen van ön?*	kehssen von ĕrn?
We will start at...	*...kor indulunk*	...korr indŏŏlŏŏnk
Ring your bell	*Csengessen!*	chan-gash-shen!
My tyre is punctured	*A kaucsukom kilyukadt [zon!*	o ko-ŏŏchŏŏkom ki-yŏŏkodt [zon!
Stop! Look out!	*Megálljon! Vigyáz-*	megahll-yon! vid-yahz-
Don't go so fast!	*Ne menjen olyan*	ne men-yen oyon dyor-
Make haste!	*Siessen! [gyorsan!*	shi-ash-shen! [shon!
We must light up [(left)	*Lámpát kell gyujtanunk [duljon*	lahmpaht kal dyŏŏytonŏŏnk [yon
Turn to the right	*Jobbra (balra) for-*	yobbro (bolro) forrdŏŏl-
Keep straight on	*Menjen egyenest előre*	men-yen ed-yanasht
Have you a road guide?	*Van uti terve?*	von ŏŏti terrva? [alerra
The one for Budapest and environs	*A Budapest és környékéről szóló*	o bŏŏdopasht ehsh kĕrrnyehkehrerl sohloh
I want my machine cleaned	*Meg akarom a gépemet tisztíttatni*	meg okorrom o gehpamat tistittotni
Where can I get my bicycle mended?	*Hol javíttathatom ki a kerékpáromat?*	hol yoveettot-hotom ki o kerrehkpahromot?
Can you repair this for me? [take?	*Ki tudja ön javítani a gépemet?*	ki tŏŏd-yo ĕrn yoveetoni o gehpamat?
How long will it	*Meddig fog tartani?*	maddig fog torrtoni?
I am a member of the English Cyclists'Touring Club	*Én tagja vagyok az Angol Kerékpár Turista Egyletnek*	ehn tog-yo vod-yok oz ongol kerrehkpahr tŏŏrishto edylatnak
Here is my ticket	*Itt a jeyyem*	itt o yad-yem

Photography. (*Fényképezés.*)

(For Vocabulary see p. 44.)

English.	Hungarian.	Pronunciation.
Must permission be obtained to photograph?	*Kell a fényképezéshez engedély?*	kal o fehnykehpazehshhaz an-gad-eh-y'?
I wish to take the interior	*Az épület belsejét kivánom levenni*	oz ehpeulat balsheyeht kivahnom lavenni
What exposure must I give?	*Meddig tegyem ki a világosságnak?*	maddig ted-yem ki o vilahgoshshahgnok?
The light is too strong	*A világitás nagyon erős*	o vilahgitahsh nod-yon a-rersh
What size of plate do you use?	*Mily nagyságú lemezeket használ?*	mi-y' nodyshahgoo lamazekat hossnahl?

English.	Hungarian.	Pronunciation.
I only use quarter-plate [room ?	*Én csak négyzet lemezeket használok*	ehn chok nehdyzat lamazekat hosnahlok[yo?
Have you a dark	*Van sötét kamarája?*	von shĕrteht komorrah-
I want to develop some plates	*Szeretnék néhány lemezt előhívni*	sa-ratnehk neh-hahny lamazt alerheevni
This plate is spoilt [exposure	*Ez a lemez el van rontva [kitéve*	az o lamaz al von rontvo [kitehva
That is due to over-	*Mert sokáig volt*	merrt shokah-ig volt
I am going to print more copies	*Lehuzok több példányt*	la-höözok tĕrbb pehldahnyt
This was spoilt in the printing	*Ez elromlott a lehuzás alatt [van*	az alromlott o la-höözahsh olott [von
It is out of focus	*A gyujtóponton kivül*	o dyooytohponton kiveul
What a beautiful photograph !	*Mily gyönyörü fénykép !*	mi-y' dyĕrn-yĕrreu fehny-kehp !
The grouping is very good	*A csoportositás nagyon jó*	o choporrtoshitahsh nod-yon yoh
I have secured some fine views	*Sikerült néhány szép felvételt csinálnom*	shikerreult neh-hahny sehp falvehtalt chinahlnom
Have you brought your camera ?	*Elhozta a fényképező gépét ?*	alhozto o fehnykehpazer gehpeht ?
Do you sell photographic materials? [quire ?	*Árul ön fényképezéshez szükséges anyagokat ?*	ahrööl ĕrn fehnykehpazehsh-haz seukshehgash on-yogokot?
What do you re-	*Mi tetszik ?*	mi tatsik ?
I want some more films	*Még néhány hártyára van szükségem*	mehg neh-hahny hahrtyahrro von seukshehg-em
I want some pretty mounts	*Szeretnék néhány csinos keretet*	sa-ratnehk neh-hahny chinosh kerratet
The lens is broken	*A lencse el van törve*	o lan-cha al von tĕrrva
The shutter doesn't act properly	*A záró nem müködik jól*	o zahroh nam miukĕrdik yohl

Religion. (*Vallás.*)

(For Vocabulary see p. 45.)

English.	Hungarian.	Pronunciation.
Is there an English church here ?	*Van itt angol templom ?*	von itt ongol tamplom?
What time is the the service ?	*Hány órakor van a szertartás ?*	hahny ohrokorr von o serrtorrtahsh ?

English.	Hungarian.	Pronunciation.
Is it far from here?	*Messze van innen?*	massa von innan?
Who is the preacher—celebrant?	*Ki prédikál?—misézik?*	ki prehdikahl?—mishehzik?
The seats are free	*A helyek szabadok*	o heyak sobodok
The seats must be paid for	*A helyekért fizetni kell*	o heyakehrrt fizatni kal
Can you find me a seat	*Tud nekem helyet szerezni?*	tööd nakem heyat sarezni?
Let us wait—go	*Várjunk — menjünk*	vahrr-jöönk — menyeunk
Pass me a hymn-book—a prayer-book	*Adjon egy énekes könyvet — imakönyvet*	od-yon edy ehnakesh kĕrnyvat—imokĕrnyvat
Mass is being celebrated	*A misét most tartják*	o misheht mosht torrtyahk
What other services are there?	*Miféle más szertartások vannak itt?*	mifehla mahsh serrtorrtahshok vonnok itt?
There is no anthem to-day	*Ma nincsen énekes szertartás*	mo ninchan ehnakesh serrtorrtahsh
The singing is beautiful	*Gyönyörűen énekelnek*	dyĕrn-yĕrrüuan ehnakelnak

The Time of Day. (*A nap szakai.*)

(For Vocabulary see pages 19—21.)

It is late	*Késő van*	kehsher von
It is not late	*Még nincs késő*	mehg ninch kehsher
It is still early	*Még korán van*	mehg korahn von
Are you tired?	*Fáradt ön?*	fahrodt ĕrn?
Not at all	*Egyáltalán nem*	ed-yahltolahn nam
Not much	*Nem nagyon*	nam nod-yon
It is only ten	*Csak tíz óra van*	chok teez ohro von
Are you sleepy?	*Álmos ön?*	ahlmosh ĕrn?
I am sleepy	*Álmos vagyok*	ahlmosh vod-yok
What time is it?	*Hány óra?*	hahny ohro?
Ten minutes past seven	*Hét óra mult tíz perccel*	heht ohro möölt teez perrts-tsal
It has just struck nine	*Éppen kilencet ütött*	ehppan kilantsat eutĕrtt
A quarter past one	*Negyed kettőkor*	nad-yad katterkorr
Half-past four	*Fél öt*	fehl ĕrt
Twenty minutes to six	*Husz perc mulva hat óra*	hööss perrts möölvo hot ohro
A quarter to eight	*Három negyed nyolc*	hahrom nad-yad nyolts
Exactly three o'clock	*Pont három óra*	pont hahrom ohro

Times, Seasons & Weather. *(Idő, évszakok és időjárás.)*

(For Vocabulary see p. 19—21.)

English.	Hungarian.	Pronunciation.
This day week	*Mához egy hétre*	mah-hoz edy hehtra
That was three or or four days ago	*Az három vagy négy nappal ezelőtt történt*	oz hahrom vody nehdy noppol azalertt tĕrr-tehnt
To-morrow fort- [night	*Holnaphoz két hétre*	holnop-hoz keht hehtra
At about this time	*Ilyen idő tájban*	i-yan ider tah-y'-bon
In a month's time	*Egy hónap mulva*	edy hohnop mŏŏlvo
The first of next month	*Jövő hónap elsején*	yĕrver hohnop alshe-yehn
At the end of this [month	*E hónap végén*	a hohnop vehg-ehn
On the last day of the month	*A hónap utolsó napján*	o hohnop ŏŏtolshoh nop-yahn
In (after) six weeks	*Hat hét mulva*	hot heht mŏŏlvo
Towards the middle of January	*Január közepe felé*	yonŏŏ-ahrr kĕrzapa faleh
In the course of a [week	*Egy hét alatt*	edy heht olott
From time to time	*Időnként*	id-ernkehnt
From one day to another	*Napról napra*	noprohl nopro
A few days ago	*Néhány nappal eze-[lőtt*	neh-hahny noppol azal-[ertt
A short time since	*Rövid idővel ezelőtt*	rĕrvid iderval azalertt
Scarcely two days ago	*Alig két napja*	olig keht nop-yo
At least a month [ago	*Legalább egy hónap-[ja*	lagolahbb edy hohnop-[yo
It is full moon	*Telehold van*	talahold von
The heat is unbearable	*A hőség tűrhetetlen*	o hershehg tĭĭrr-hatat-lan
I am very warm	*Nagyon melegem van*	nod-yon malag-em von
I am afraid it will rain	*Attól félek, esni fog*	ottohl fehlak, ashni fog
We shall have a [storm	*Vihar lesz*	vi-horr less
Did you see the lightning?	*Látta a villámlást*	lahtto o villahm-lahsht
I heard the thunder	*Hallottam a menny-[dörgést*	hollottom o manny-[dĕrrg-ehsht
How it pours!	*Hogy szakad az eső!*	hody sokod oz asher!
I am wet through	*Egészen átáztam*	ag-ehssan ahtahztom
Would you like an umbrella?	*Adjak esernyőt?*	od-yok ashern-yert?
Look at the rain-[bow	*Nézze a szivárványt*	nehzza o sivahrvahnyt

English.	Hungarian.	Pronunciation.
It is growing very cold [here	*Nagyon hideg kezd lenni [tél*	nod-yon hidag kazd lenni [tehl
Winter will soon be	*Nemsokára itt lesz a*	namshokahro itt less o
It snows	*Havazik*	hovozik
It freezes; it thaws	*Fagy; olvad*	fod*y*; olvod
It is very dirty	*Nagy a sár*	nod*y* o shahrr
It is very windy	*Nagy a szél*	nod*y* o sehl
How high the wind is! [east	*Hogy fuj a szél!*	hod*y* fŏŏy o sehl
The wind is in the	*Keletről fuj a szél*	kalatre*r*l fŏŏy o sehl
The dust is terrible	*Rettentő por van*	rettante*r* porr von
I hope it will be fine [day!	*Remélem, szép idő lesz [nap!*	ramehlem, sehp ide*r* less [nop!
What a beautiful	*Milyen gyönyörü*	mi-yan d*y*e*r*n-yĕ*r*reŭ

Post, Telegraph and Telephone.

(*Póstahivatal, táviratok és telefon.*)

(For Vocabulary see p. 52.)

Customs declara-	*Áru-bevallás*	ahrŏŏ-bavollahsh
Number of — [tion	*A vámjegy száma*	o vahm-yad*y* sahmo
Nature of contents	*Mit tartalmaz?*	mit torrtolmoz?
Value of contents	*Mi az értéke?*	mi oz ehrrtehka?
Place of destination	*Hova megy?*	hovvo med*y*?
Stamp of office of origin [of sender	*Vám hivatal bélyege [címe*	vahm hivotol beh-yegą [tseema
Name and address	*A küldő neve és*	o keŭlde*r* nava ehsh
Signature of sender	*A küldő aláirása*	o keŭlde*r* olah-irahshǫ
Where is the post (telegraph) office?	*Hol van a pósta-hivatal (távíró)?*	hol von o pohshto-hivotol (tahveeroh)?
Have you any letters for Mr. N.?	*Van levél N. úr részére?*	von lavehl N. oorr rehssehra?
Will this letter go to-night?	*Elmegy ez a levél még ma este?*	almed*y* az o lavehl mehg mo ashta?
What stamp will this letter require?	*Mennyi bélyeg kell reá? [levelet*	mann-yi beh-yeg kal re-ah? [lavalat
To register a letter	*Ajánlva küldeni a*	o-yahnlvo keŭldani o
I wish to send a telegram	*Sürgönyözni szeretnék*	sheŭrrghĕ*r*n-yĕ*r*zni sarat-nehk
What is the cost of the telegram?	*Mennyibe kerül egy sürgöny?*	mann-yiba kerreŭl ed*y* sheŭrrghĕ*r*ny?
When does the mail leave for England?	*Mikor indul Angliába a levélpósta?*	mikorr indŏŏl ongliahbo o lavehlpohshto?

English.	Hungarian.	Pronunciation.
Is the London mail in yet?	*Megérkezett már a londoni levélpósta?*	meg-ehrkazatt mahr o londoni lavehlpohshto?
When is the next delivery?	*Mikor van a legközelebbi levél kihordás?*	mikorr von o lagkĕrzalabbi lavehl kihorrdahsh?
The latest delivery is at...	*Az utolsó levél kihordás ... órakor van*	oz ŏŏtolshoh lavehl kihorrdahsh...ohrokorr von
I want a money order for ...	*Kérnék egy póstautalványt...*	kehrnehk edy pohshtoŏŏtolvahnyt...
Payable at the G.P.O., London	*Fizetendő a londoni főpóstán*	fizatander o londoni ferpohshtahn
Are you on the telephone?	*Van az ön házánál telefon?*	von oz ĕrn hahzahnahl telefon?
What is your number?	*Mi a száma?*	mi o sahmo?
My number is...	*... a számom*	... o sahmom
Will you ring me up?	*Hívni fog a telefonhoz?*	heevni fog o telefonhoz?
The Telephone Exchange	*A telefon központ*	o telefon kĕrz-pont
Line engaged	*Mással beszél*	mahsh-shol bassehl
Are you there?	*Ott van ön?*	ott von ĕrn?
Who are you?	*Ki beszél?*	ki bassehl?

Correspondence. (*Levelezés.*)

(For Vocabulary see p. 53.)

English.	Hungarian.	Pronunciation.
I must write a letter	*Levelet kell irnom*	lavalat kal irrnom
I want some paper	*Kérek levélpapirost*	kehrek lavehl-popirosht
Have you any?	*Van önnek?*	von ĕrnnak?
Will you give me some?	*Adhat belőle?*	od-hot bal-er-la?
Lend me a sheet	*Adjon egy ívet, kérem*	od-yon edy iv-at, kehrem
A quire	*Egy koncot*	edy kontsot
Do you like a hard or soft pen?	*Puha vagy kemény tollat használ ön?*	pŏŏ-ho vody kamehny tollot hossnahl ĕrn?
I like it hard, broad	*Kemény, széles, tollat használok*	kamehny, sehlesh, tollot hossnahlok
Is your letter for the post?	*Van önnek a póstára vinni való levele?*	von ĕrnnak o pohshtahro vinni voloh lavala?
What is the day of the month?	*Hányadika van ma?*	hahn-yodiko von mo?

English.	Hungarian.	Pronunciation.
To-day is the third	*Ma harmadika van*	mo horrmodiko von [lat
Seal your letter	*Pecsételje le a levelet*	patchehtal-ya le o lava
There is no sealing-wax	*Nincsen pecsétviaszom*	ninchan patchehtviossom
Take this letter to the post	*Vigye ezt a levelet a póstára*	vid-ya azt a lavalat o pohshtahro
Pay the postage	*Tegyen bélyeget reá*	ted-yen beh-yagat re-ah

Legal and Judicial Phrases.

(*Jogi és törvénykezési kifejezések.*)

(For Vocabulary see p. 47.)

English.	Hungarian.	Pronunciation.
Call the police	*Hívjon rendőrt*	heev-yon renderrt
I give this man in charge	*Ezt az embert elfogatom*	azt oz ambert alfogotom
What do you charge him with?	*Mivel vádolja?*	mival vahdol-yo?
He has stolen my purse [watch	*Ellopta a tárcámat mat*	allopto o tahrtsahmot
He has taken my	*Ellopta az órámat*	allopto oz ohrahmot
Where is the police-station? [nesses?	*Hol a rendőrállomás?*	hol o renderrahllomahsh?
Have you any wit-	*Van tanúja?*	von tonoo-yo?
I have two witnesses	*Két tanúm van*	keht tonoom von
Where is the court?	*Hol a törvényszék?*	hol o těrrvehnysehk?
Do you wish to prosecute?	*Kíván pört indítani?*	kivahn pěrrt indeetoni?
I don't care to prosecute [vise?	*Nem kívánok pört indítani*	nam kivahnok pěrrt indeetoni
What do you ad-	*Mit tanácsol?*	mit tonahchol?
What am I to do?	*Mit tegyek?*	mit ted-yek?
Can you recommend a solicitor?	*Ajánlhatna ügyvédet?*	o-yahnl-hotno eüdyvehdet?
Will you take up my case?	*Elvállalja az ügyemet?*	alvahllol-yo oz eüdyamat?
Can I have an interpreter?	*Kaphatok tolmácsot?*	kop-hotok tolmahchot?
I want bail	*Jótállást kívánok*	yohtahllahsht kivahnok
Send to my friends	*Küldjön el az ismerőseimhez*	keüld-yěrn al oz ishmerrěrsheym-haz

English.	Hungarian.	Pronunciation.
Where is the British Embassy?—Consulate?	*Hol van az angol nagykövetség?—konzulátus?*	hol von oz ongol nodykĕrvatshehg?—konzŏŏlahtŏŏsh?
This is quite wrong	*Ez helytelen*	az heytalan
It is not just	*Ez nem igazságos*	az nam igoz-shahgosh
It was all a mistake	*Tévedés volt az egész*	tehvadehsh volt oz agehss
I apologise	*Bocsánatot kérek*	botchahnotot kehrek
I accept your apology	*Elfogadom a bocsánatkérést*	alfogodom o botchahnotkehrehsht
I claim damages	*Kárpótlást követelek*	kahrpohtlahsht kĕrvatalek
The case is adjourned until...	*Az esetet ... ig elnapolják*	oz ashatet...ig alnopolyahk
I will be here	*Itt leszek*	itt lessek

Commercial & Trading. (*Kereskedelem.*)

(For Vocabulary see p. 49.)

Send in my account	*Küldje a számlámat*	keüld-ya o sahmlahmot
There is an error in your account	*Hiba van a számlában*	hibo von o sahmlahbon
You have overcharged me	*Többet számított mint kellene*	tĕrbbat sahmeetott mint kallana
This has been paid	*Ezt már kifizettem*	azt mahrr kifizattam
Your account is overdue	*Az ön számlája már rég esedékes*	oz ĕrn sahmlah-yo mahr rehg ashadehkesh
Give me a receipt	*Adjon nyugtát*	od-yon nyŏŏgtaht
The firm has failed	*A cég megbukott*	o tsehg megbŏŏkott
What assets are there?	*Milyen a vagyoni helyzet?*	mi-yan o vod-yoni heyzet?
Show me a balance-sheet	*Mutassa a vagyonmérleget*	mŏŏtoshsho o vod-yonmehrlag-et
My samples are delayed	*A minták késtek*	o mintahk kehshtak
I want to get them through the custom-house	*A vámház utján szeretném megkapni*	o vahm-hahz ŏŏt-yahn sa-rat-nehm megkopni
I claim damages	*Kárpotlást kérek*	kahrpotlahsht kehrek
Can I insure my luggage?	*Biztosíthatom a podgyászomat?*	biztosheet-hotom o podd-yahsomot?
What is the rate?	*Mit kell fizetni?*	mit kal fizatni?
Your luggage is liable to duty	*A podgyásza vámolás alá kerül*	o podd-yahsso vahmolahsh olah kerrĭul

English.	Hungarian.	Pronunciation.
Will you accept a bill?	*Elfogadja ön ezt a váltót?*	alfogod-yo ĕrn azt o vahltoht?
At three months	*Három hónapra*	hahrom hohnopro
This cheque needs endorsing	*Ezt a cheque-et alá kell irni*	azt o chek-et olah kal irrni
Quote me a price	*Mondja meg az árát*	mond-yo meg oz ahrraht
Pack the goods well	*Jól csomagolja be a tárgyakat* [*tal*	yohl chomogol-yo ba o tahrd-yokot [tol
Send by fast train	*Küldje gyors vonat-*	kĕuld-ya dyorrsh vonot-
What dividend is declared?	*Mennyi osztalékot adnak?*	mann-yi ostolehkot od-nok?
I have a letter of introduction	*Van ajánló levelem*	von o-yahnloh lavalam
Give me your estimate	*Csináljon költség vetést*	chinahl-yon kĕrltshehg-vatehsht

Changing Money. (*Pénsváltás.*)

Where can I get money changed?	*Hol lehet pénzt váltatni?*	hol le-hat pehnzt vahltotni
I want change for a £5 note	*Egy ötfontos bankjegyet szeretnék felváltatni*	edy ĕrtfontosh bonk-yad-yet sa-rat-nehk falvahltotni
Will you give me Hungarian money?	*Kérem, adjon magyar pénzt*	kehrem, od-yon mod-yorr pehnzt
What is the equivalent in English money?	*Mennyi ez angol pénzben?*	mann-yi az ongol pehnzban?
Will you change me these sovereigns?	*Kérem, váltsa fel ezeket az aranyokat*	kehrem, vahltsho fal az-ekat oz orron-yokot
Will you cash this cheque for me?	*Kérem, váltsa be ezt a cheque-et*	kehrem, vahltsho ba azt o chek-et

MONEY. (*Pénz.*)

The Hungarian monetary unit is the Pengö, which is the equivalent of 100 Fillér. Par value is 27.825 pengös per £1.

The following approximate equivalents are calculated on the par values of the £ and $. The actual rate of exchange is subject to fluctuation.

Hungarian Money with English and American Values.

NOTES.

Hungarian	English	American
1,000 pengö	=£35 18 9	=174·68
100 „	3 11 10	17·46
50 „	1 15 11	8·73
20 „	14 4	3·48
10 „	7 2	1·74
5 „	3 7	0·87

SILVER

Hungarian	English	American
1 pengö	= 8½d.	= 0·17 cents

NICKEL.

Hungarian	English	American
50 Fillér	= 4¼d.	= 0·08 cents
20 „	1¾d.	0·03 „
10 „	1d.	0·02 „

COPPER.

Hungarian	English	American
2 Fillér	= ¼d.	= —
1 „	—	—

English and American Money with Hungarian Values.

English	American	Hungarian
£50 0 0	=$243·00	=pengö 1391·25
25 0 0	121·50	695·62
10 0 0	48·60	278·25
5 0 0	24·30	139·12
1 0 0	4·86	27·825
10s. 0d.	= $2·43	=pengö 13·91
5s. 0d.	1·21	6·95
2s. 6d.	0·60	3·48
1s. 0d.	0·24	1·39
6d.	0·12	0·70
1d.	0·02	0·12

WEIGHTS & MEASURES. (*Mértékek.*)

The Metric system is used throughout Hungary.

MEASURES OF LENGTH. (*Hosszmértékek.*)

English	Hungarian
1 inch ...	=2·5399 *centiméter*
1 foot (12 in.)	= 30 *centiméter*
1 yard (3 ft.)	= 91 *centiméter*
1 furlong (220 yds.)	=201 *méter*
1 mile (1760 yds.)	=1 *kilom.* 610 *m.*
5 miles ...	= 8 *kilométer*

Hungarian	English
1 *centiméter*	= 0·394 in.
30 *centiméter*	= 1 foot
1 *méter*	= 1·093 yds. (39·37 in.)
1 *hectométer*	= 109 yds. 1 ft.
1 *kilométer*	= 1093 yds. 5 ft.
5 *kilométer*	=3 miles 220 yds.

WEIGHTS. (*Sulymértékek.*)

English.		Hungarian.	Hungarian.		English.
1 ounce	=	28 *gramm*	1 *gramm*	=	0·0357 oz.
8 oz. (½ lb.)	=	227 *gramm*	100 *gramm*	=	3½ oz.
1 lb. (16 oz.)	=	453 *gramm*	½ *kilo.* (500 *gm.*)	=	1·1 lb.
1 qr. (28 lb.)	=	12 *kilo.* 690 *gm.*	1 *kilo.* (1000 *gm.*)	=	2·2046 lb.
1 cwt. (112 lb.)	=	50 *kilo.* 750 *gm.*	5 *kilogramm*	=	11 lb.
1 ton (20 cwt.)	=	1015 *kilo.*	1000 *kilo.*	=	19 cwt. 2 qrs. 23 lb.

LIQUIDS. (*Űrmértékek.*)

English.		Hungarian.	Hungarian.		English.
1 pint ...	=	0·57 *liter*	1 *liter*	=	1·76 pints (0·220 gal.)
1 quart (2 pts.)	=	1·14 *liter*	5 *liter*	=	1 gallon 1 pint.
1 gallon (4 qts.)	=	4·5434 *liter*	100 *liter*	=	22 gallons
1 peck (2 gals.)	=	9 *liter*	1 *hectoliter*	=	2·751 bushels
1 bushel (8 gals.)	=	36 *liter*	100 *hectoliter*	=	34 qrs. 3·121 bus.

POSTAL RATES.

The rates of postage from Hungary to Great Britain and the United States of America are as follows:—

LETTERS.—25 fillér per 20 gramm, and 15 fillér for each additional 20 gramm or part thereof.

POST CARDS.—10 fillér; reply-paid cards, 20 fillér.

PRINTED PAPERS (max. weight 2,000 gramm).—5 fillér per 50 gramm.

COMMERCIAL PAPERS (max. weight 2,000 gramm).—5 fillér per 50 gramm. Minimum charge 25 fillér.

The Internal rates in Hungary are:—

LETTERS.—10 fillér for 20 gramm; 20 fillér for 250 gramm.

POST CARDS.—5 fillér; reply 10 fillér.

PRINTED PAPERS.—Not exceeding 50 gramm, 3 fillér; 100 gramm, 5 fillér; 250 gramm, 10 fillér; 500 gramm, 20 fillér.

COMMERCIAL PAPERS.—Not exceeding 250 gramm, 10 fillér; 500 gramm, 20 fillér.

PARCELS.—1 kilo., 30 fillér; 3 kilo., 75 fillér; 5 kilo., 75 fillér. 15 fillér for each additional ½ kilo.

Up to 150 kilo., for each kilo. 12 fillér; minimum 60 fillér.
Over 150 kilo., ,, ,, 24 fillér; ,, 60 fillér.

TELEGRAMS *from* Hungary *to* Great Britain, 60 fillér tax and 24 fillér per word.

INLAND telegraph rates in Hungary, 60 fillér for first 10 words; 6 fillér for each additional word.